The YADA YADA Celebrations and Recipes

Neta Jackson

CASTLE ROCK CREATIVE
Evanston, Illinois 60202

Published in Evanston, Illinois. Castle Rock Creative.

ISBN: 978-0-9982107-5-9

Cover photo and design: Dave Jackson
Illustrations: ChrisGorgio; Epine_Art; RamanaVenkat; topform84; Vecteezy.com | iStock

Printed in the United States of America

For a complete list of
books by Dave and Neta Jackson visit
www.daveneta.com
www.riskinggrace.com
www.trailblazerbooks.com

Dedication

To the forty sisters who at one time or another

have been a part of the women's Bible study

that originally inspired the

Yada Yada Prayer Group series

and all the Yada Yada-related novels

that grew out of it.

God has used you to

change me

more than you'll ever know.

Contents

SECTION 1—*Celebrations through the Year*

SECTION 2—*Anytime Celebrations*

SECTION 3—Recipes from *The Yada Yada Prayer Group*

Recipes from *The Yada Yada Prayer Group Gets Down*

Recipes from *The Yada Yada Prayer Group Gets Real*

Recipes from *The Yada Yada Prayer Group Gets Tough*

---

* **Bonus** (not previously included)

Recipes from *The Yada Yada Prayer Group Gets Caught*

Recipes from *The Yada Yada Prayer Group Gets Rolling*

---

* **Bonus** (not previously included)

Recipes from *The Yada Yada Prayer Group Gets Decked Out*

"Yada Yada"?

What in the world does that mean?

YADA . . . A Hebrew word found in the Hebrew Old Testament 944 times.

A root word meaning "to know"—with many varied meanings and applications.

But basically "YADA" means: "to know and be known . . . intimately."

Psalm 139 could be called The Yada Psalm—how intimately God knows us. In the Hebrew version of this psalm, the word "yada" appears numerous times.

Thus, The Yada Yada Prayer Group was born! A desire to know God and be known by God intimately—and to know each other intimately as well.

Introduction

Hey, Yada Yada Sisters . . . This Book Is for You!

Time to get out your crazy colored socks and your dancing shoes and your favorite cooking pot and—

Oh, wait. Maybe I should say something about why we put together this ***Yada Yada Celebrations and Recipes*** book.

As many readers of the Yada Yada Prayer Group novels know, the Yada Yada sisters were always celebrating something. And cooking food. As I followed these feisty women around through all seven novels, I thought: *Wouldn't it be great to collect and expand these multi-cultural celebrations and recipes into a book, so readers—and even those dear souls who haven't read the novels—could enjoy them with their families and friends too?*

We first did a "Party Edition" of the Yada Yada series, with relevant celebrations and recipes in the back of each book. But not everyone who'd already read the novels wanted to buy the new edition—and besides, who actually remembers which celebration or recipe appeared in which book? (And who wants to get food splatters on your favorite Yada Yada novel?)

So . . . ta da! Here they are! All the celebrations and recipes in one book!

Sections 1 and 2

The first section includes **"Celebrations through the Year."** The second section features **"Anytime Celebrations."** Most of these showed up in the Yada Yada Prayer Group novels, but we've added a few more, all collected and expanded into practical ideas you can use with your kiddos, your prayer group buddies, your church folks, or as a way to reach out to your neighbors—year-round!

Section 3

The third section begins with the Yada Yada Prayer Group's **"Signature Recipes"** from each of the Yada Yada sisters starting on page 72! Also, to the recipes for each book, we've added new bonus recipes that didn't appear in the original Party Editions. No need to wait for a celebration to try these gems—some for every day, some for special occasions.

Because you know, a true Yada Yada loves to eat!

A Word about Multi-Cultural Celebrations . . .

Because the Yada Yada Prayer Group novels include a cast of characters from several different ethnic and racial groups, the sisters enjoyed learning about celebrations (and food!) from various cultural traditions. We hope you do, too.

But what celebrations to include in this expanded collection has been a bit of a challenge. Some, like **Kwanzaa**, a fairly recent holiday which celebrates African heritage for African-Americans, was originally developed in 1966 as a non-religious "alternative" to Christmas. *Whoa.* Should we include it?

At the same time, how different is that from the secular (non-religious) aspects of our own favorite holiday: **Christmas**. Santa Claus, mega-spending on gifts, office parties, Frosty the Snowman, Christmas trees, even favorite movies like "It's a Wonderful Life" and "A Christmas Carol" that never mention Jesus, even though they're uplifting stories about the "spirit of Christmas." Many (most?) Christian families not only celebrate the true meaning of Christmas—the birth of Jesus, the promised Messiah—with Christmas carols and pageants and reading the Christmas story from the Gospel of Luke, but they also enjoy many of the more secular trappings surrounding this "magical holiday."

Or **Halloween**. When our kids were young, our church hosted a Harvest Party on or near Halloween as an alternative to the more ghoulish aspects of this holiday (ghosts, witches, slasher movies, etc.). But I will be the first to admit that I loved dressing up in costume as a kid (nothing scary) and going trick-or-treating. Later, as a Mom, I took our children trick-or-treating too, encouraging homemade costumes and sometimes dressing up ourselves in parent/child "pairs" (e.g. Raggedy Ann and Andy; Red Riding Hood and the Wolf). Harmless fun. Now that we have an empty nest, I always make sure I'm home on Halloween to answer the door and be a friendly adult welcoming the neighborhood children, admiring their costumes, giving out glow bracelets. Historically, however, "Halloween" is actually a bad translation of "All Hallow's Eve," the evening before All Saints Day (November 1)—a religious holiday many of us Protestants don't know anything about and rarely celebrate.

And then there's **St. Patrick's Day**—especially in Chicago. Everybody wears green, the city dyes the Chicago River green, there are big parades, we eat corned-beef-and-cabbage (oh, yum!), schools decorate with four-leaf-clovers and leprechauns, the radio plays "Danny Boy," and, yes, many people use it as an excuse to drink lots and lots of beer. Largely ignored is the fact that St. Patrick was a Christian missionary to Ireland.

All this to say, most of us already mix-and-match our holiday celebrations, picking out what's compatible with our faith and/or what's "good" and "innocent fun" from the secular versions, and ignoring the rest.

What's important to keep in mind when deciding what new celebrations to add to your personal or family life is this:

- Celebrations can be an important way to learn about other cultures and ethnic groups.
- Celebrating *with* people from other cultures, participating in a holiday that's important to their life experience, can be an important way to "break down barriers" and develop new friendships.
- Remember that our own familiar celebrations often include a combination of religious and secular customs that have evolved over time . . . so don't be quick to judge.
- But do feel free to sort through the various ways to celebrate a particular holiday and choose what is meaningful to you and your faith and family.

So . . . enjoy!

Neta

NOTE: Readers of the Yada Yada Prayer Group novels (seven in all) will recognize the names of favorite characters that appear in this Celebrations and Recipes book. If you haven't met these characters yet—and they *are* characters in every sense of the word!—you may want to meet them in the books themselves. See the ad pages in the back for more about these novels—or go to www.daveneta.com.

Section 1
Celebrations through the Year

New Year's Eve

The beginning of a New Year is celebrated all over our globe—though not all countries celebrate on December 31. China and Israel, for example, have calendars based on a lunar month, so the date of their New Year celebrations, while consistent on a lunar calendar, change on the "standard" solar calendar most of us use.

Many of us remember the New Year's Eve not too long ago when the calendar flipped from 1999 to 2000—the second millennium was here! Wahoo! What an historical event! (Though, to be honest, the next day pretty much resembled the one just before it. The sun rose, the sun set, in that wonderful rhythm of God's awesome creation.)

A Little Background

Undoubtedly, people have commemorated New Year's Eve ever since primitive calendars were able to identify the date. But Christian "Watch Night" services seem to have begun with the Moravians, a small community of believers in Bohemia (now the Czech Republic) in the eighteenth century. These Christians, persecuted because of their protests against a state church and its many excesses, fled to Bohemia and eventually to the New World in search of freedom to worship God according to what they believed was the New Testament model. In 1733, they held their first Watch Night service, a time to give thanks to God for His blessing and protection in the year past, and to rededicate themselves to God's service in the coming year.

John Wesley borrowed the idea for his followers who were later known as Methodists. Since then, many modern Christians have observed some sort of New Year's Eve service reflecting on God's goodness during the past year and recommitting themselves to Him for the New Year. Two biblical themes are often emphasized: Jesus' words before His betrayal, "*Watch and pray* so that you will not fall into temptation" (Matthew 26:41, NIV; emphasis added) and His warning to be ready for His return at the end of the age, "Therefore *keep watch*, because you do not know the day or the hour" (Matthew 25:13, NIV; emphasis added).

However, African-American Christians experienced special significance in this observance on the night of December 31, 1862, which for them was also "Freedom's Eve"—the night before the Emancipation Proclamation went into effect and all the slaves in the Confederate states were declared free. As they came together in churches and private homes all across the nation, hope, fear, and prayers gave way to shouts of joy, songs, and thanksgiving to God when word spread after midnight that the Proclamation had not been retracted. It's an event that all Christians can incorporate into their Watch Night services, praising God for bringing us through another year and thanking Him for both physical and spiritual freedom.

A Watch Night Celebration

If your usual New Year's Eve consists of sacking out in front of the TV and watching "the ball" fall in Times Square . . . or leaving the kids with a babysitter while you hold a glass of bubbly and sing "Auld Lang Syne" at the office party . . . consider celebrating a family-friendly Watch Night. The following Watch Night celebration can be adapted for use in a church setting or at home with family and friends.

Invite!

- "Make new friends, but keep the old . . . " as the old camp song goes. A New Year's Eve celebration is an excellent time to celebrate "old friends" and "new." A youth group from one church could invite a youth group from another church. A family could invite another family—or two! One "old friends" and one "new."
- It's important to keep our children's hearts—and our own—open to those Jesus loves but are often overlooked. "Birds of a feather flock together" is *not* in the Bible!

Eat!

- Begin the evening with a potluck meal. If your church or neighborhood involves many racial or ethnic groups, this could be an "international night" with foods from different countries. What fun!
- If done at home with family and friends, plan a festive meal for which various participants help prepare different dishes.

Play!

- After the meal, play games that adults and youth can play together—relays, guessing games, ice breakers, or favorite board games.
- Play charades . . . but instead of using the traditional categories of book title, movie title, song, etc., pantomime events from the preceding year with which everyone is familiar. Agree on categories such as *Happy Event* (demonstrated by pulling one's mouth into a grin with fingers), *Sad Event* (pull mouth down into a frown),

Crazy Event (circling fingers around ears), *Scary Event* (holding eyes exceptionally wide with fingers), *God's Provision* (fingers raked down over one's head like falling rain), etc. Other gestures may follow the game's typical sign language. (Google "charades" on the Internet for examples.) No words or sounds may be spoken. No letters may be "drawn" in the air to spell out a word. Rather than dividing into teams, each player can take a turn portraying an event while everyone else guesses. Little ones may need an adult's help.

New Year Resolutions or Goals

- Setting a few goals for the coming year can be fun and encouraging, if it doesn't rise out of guilt or pressure from others.
- Pass out a 5 x 7 sheet of paper to both kids and adults. Each one should write down three things they'd like to do in the coming year. Don't tell anyone what you write down!
- **Areas to consider:** Something fun I'd like to do (for example: "Participate in a local 5K"); Books I'd like to read (e.g., "*The Lord of the Ring*" series or "A new book every month"); A new skill to learn (e.g., "Learn how to bake bread" or "Learn to change a tire"); Someone I'd like to get to know (e.g., "Invite three neighbors to go out for coffee" or "Sit beside a new kid at school"); Set a new goal in a sport or activity (e.g., "Decrease my golf score by 5 strokes" or "Beat my personal 5K time by 5 minutes"); Serve others (e.g., "Volunteer at the local elementary school to read to kids" or "Sign up to deliver Meals on Wheels"). No one should be forced to do this—keep it voluntary and fun.
- It might also be fun to add three "predictions" for the coming year: E.g., So-and-so is going to win the local election; we are going to get X number of inches of snow this winter; Uncle Wallace will finally get rid of his old car . . . or whatever!
- Goals should be *reasonable* and *measurable.* (Not "I am going to act more mature this year." Hmm. What exactly would that mean?)
- Fold the 5 x 7 papers so no one else can see them. Write your name on the outside. Put them all in a jar . . . and open them *next* New Year's Eve to see how many goals or predictions were met.
- Be sure to *not* belittle anyone who doesn't meet their goal(s). Maybe it wasn't realistic. Unmet goals can simply be renewed for next year—or tossed and replaced with something more realistic or a new challenge.

Reflect!

- Before midnight arrives, explain some of

the history of Watch Night services as mentioned earlier in the "Background" section. Read Mark 13:28–37, in which Jesus told how we can recognize when the time for His return is approaching and encouraged us to be ready by watching and praying. (You may want to use the New King James Version, which uses that language.)

Sing!

- Sing songs about God's faithfulness, either from a hymnal or some of the contemporary praise and worship songs.

Commit!

- Invite individuals to renew their commitment to the Lord as they prepare to enter the New Year. This could be a spontaneously worded commitment with a particular focus, or, for the younger ones, it might reiterate these words from Joshua 24:15: "As for me and my household, we will serve the LORD" (NIV).
- As each person makes a commitment, let him or her light a candle and put it in a candleholder on a table *OR* plant it in a bed of sand in a large pan. The more candles, the brighter the light.

Bless!

- An alternative (or an addition) might be to pray blessings on the children and teenagers as the parents light a candle for each one. For inspiration, read **Mark 10:13–16**, imagining what Jesus might have said as He took the children into His arms, placed His hands on their heads, and blessed them.

Ring in the New Year!

- At midnight, ring in the New Year by letting everyone ring a bell, jingle keys, shake a tambourine, or tap lightly on a glass with a spoon.
- Conclude the evening by singing, "This Little Light of Mine." Sing all the usual verses and make up your own: *"All around my neighborhood / With all my friends / Every day in school / When I go to work,* etc. . . . *I'm going to let it shine! Let it shine, let it shine, let it shine!"*

NOTE: Different cultures celebrate the New Year at different times of year and in different ways. We're including two of them in this book—the Chinese New Year (which falls in January or February on our calendar) and the Jewish New Year, called Rosh Hashanah, which happens in the Fall. (See page 24.)

Chinese New Year Celebration

According to the U.S. census, there are 3.79 million Chinese living in the U.S., many of them citizens. Of these, 2.2 million were born in China. Most large cities in the U.S. have a "Chinatown" featuring Chinese cuisine, celebrations, and culture. And you don't have to look far to find Chinese students at most colleges and universities. If you're fortunate, you may have a Chinese co-worker or neighbor, or a Chinese believer in your women's Bible study. (I did!)

The Chinese New Year—also known as the Spring Festival—is a major celebration in China, a special time for families to get together. But for many Chinese in the U.S., there's a good chance their families are back in China. Many would enjoy celebrating with friends here, teaching you about their traditions, and sharing what they're missing "back home."

When is the Chinese New Year?

Chinese New Year celebrations start on the 23rd day of the 12th lunar month of the Chinese calendar and end on the 15th day of the first lunar month. It's easy to go online and find the corresponding date of any particular year in our own calendar.

The Chinese Twelve-Year Cycle

For the Chinese, years are further classified by a scheme that assigns an animal and its reputed attributes to each year in a repeating twelve-year cycle. (Note the images across the top of the page.)

Knowing that 2018 is the Year of the Dog, for instance, shows your Chinese friends that you care about them and their culture. You could ask a Chinese friend what animal year they are (the year they were born) and if that meant anything to them growing up.

Preparation

Because visiting various family members during the New Year is the major activity, the house gets a thorough cleaning. Red banners saying "Happy Chinese New Year" are hung on the front door. If it's the Year of the Dog, for instance, there are stuffed dogs, paper cutouts of dogs, plastic dogs, dogs on banners, etc. all over the place!

Food

In the north, **dumplings** with a special vinegar sauce is the traditional specialty. Here in the U.S. they are usually available in the frozen section of the grocery store.

In the south, **sticky rice cake** is a special treat.

Traditional Greeting

In Chinese, *Xin nian kuai le* means "Happy New Year."

Visiting

On the Eve of Chinese New Year, the celebrations begin! Usually you visit with the husband's family on New Year's Eve and on Day 1.

On Day 2, you visit the wife's family.

On Days 3-7, you visit other relatives.

On Day 8, you go back to work!

Visitors usually bring fruit, special foods, and red envelopes with money for the children. Basically, everyone sits around and chats, munching on sunflower seeds until the food is ready.

Those Red Envelopes

It's traditional to give **red envelopes with money** to children under eighteen.

How to Celebrate with Your Chinese Friends

Practice saying *"Xin nian kuai le,"* pronounced: *Sheen neean kwai luh.*("Happy New Year"). Look up a translation program online to find out how to pronounce the Chinese words.

An American missionary to China told us, "When we are celebrating with our Chinese friends, we give red envelopes with money (or McDonalds coupons!) to the children, share a meal with them, and just hang out. We also bring a simple gift with us—either a food gift, flowers, fruit, or something I have baked."

Purim—The Feast of Lots

Purim falls in mid-winter, sometime in February or March. (Observed on the fourteenth day of the Hebrew month of Adar.)

Also considered a Feast of Joy, Purim is a celebration of God's deliverance of the Jews from an evil plot to exterminate them during their captivity in Persia. The entire story is told in the Book of Esther, a plot with more twists and turns than a bestselling novel or Oscar-winning movie.

Meaning for Christians:

As with all stories of God's deliverance in the Bible, this story is prophetic of God sending us a Savior to deliver us from our sinful condition and to restore God's people to their rightful place as heirs of God's kingdom. There is also a personal dimension, of recognizing that God uses ordinary people to do extraordinary things for Him. As Mordecai said to Esther: "Who knows but that you have come to royal position for such a time as this?" (Esther 4:14, NIV).

Ways to Celebrate:

Read or tell the story dramatically from the Book of Esther.

It's fun to dress up! Either in your own family (each person might have to play several roles) or with a group of children, dress up in costumes and act out the parts as the story is told: Esther, Uncle Mordecai, the King, Queen Vashti, Haman, the two plotters who wanted to kill the king, heralds and messengers and ladies-in-waiting.

Make "graggers" (noisemakers) for children to shake, rattle, or whirl whenever the evil Haman's name is mentioned. Marbles inside clean, empty juice cans that have been decorated and resealed can be shaken with

Jewish Holy Days and Festivals

In *The Yada Yada Prayer Group Gets Down* (Book 2), Ruth Garfield, a Messianic Jew, invited some of the Yada Yada sisters to attend one of the Jewish High Holy Days at her Messianic congregation. During the service, the leader explained the meaning of various "feasts of remembrance" instituted in the Old Testament, and also how they prophetically pointed toward the coming of the Messiah.

Scattered throughout this Celebration book, we are including several of these important Jewish Holy Days and Festivals, falling generally in the time of year they take place:

- **Purim—The Feast of Lots (this page)**
- **Passover—and a Christian Seder (page 14)**
- **Rosh Hashanah—Jewish New Year (page 24)**
- **Yom Kippur—Day of Atonement (page 25)**
- **Sukkot—The Feast of Booths (page 26)**

delightful (!) noise. Or buy real graggers online or at a Jewish supply store.

A fun song for pre-schoolers can be sung to the tune "B-I-N-G-O": "There is a holiday I love, and Purim is its name-o! P-U-R-I-M . . . ."

Other ideas can be found online at www.biblicalholidays.com. Or Google "Purim" and find a number of online sites with activities and recipes—especially for the jam-filled **Hamentashen Cookies**, which are supposed to resemble the triangular shape of Hamen's hat!

The Lenten Season

I didn't grow up observing Lent, the forty days from Ash Wednesday until Easter. It was something Catholics and some liturgical Protestant churches did—Anglicans, Methodists, Lutherans, Orthodox. But in my adult years, I was introduced to the concept as even some evangelical and Anabaptist churches observed Lent.

What Is Lent?

The word is a shortened version of "Lenten," related to the Old English word, *lencten*, or "spring," also related to the word "long"—perhaps referring to the lengthening of the days as spring arrives.

Like Advent leading up to Christmas (see page 38), Lent is a time set aside as preparation for Holy Week, which includes Palm Sunday, Good Friday, and Easter (Resurrection Sunday!), the high point of the Christian year. Forty days to remember Christ's forty days of fasting and prayer in the wilderness, a time to reflect on Christ's sacrifice for us. A time for prayer, confession, and repentance.

Observing Lent

For many who observe Lent, it's also a time for sacrificing something—giving up TV or dessert or the internet or alcohol or whatever seems to have an untoward hold on one's life. Some may choose fasting from one meal a day, or one day out of the week. Hopefully to give more time to read the Gospels, reflect on the life of Jesus, and give thanks for God's awesome gift of salvation.

A sacrifice of . . .

Recently, Ash Wednesday and Valentine's Day landed on the same date—February 14—leading to frequent jokes and even melodramatic angst about how to celebrate two such disparate holidays: Ash Wednesday, a solemn day beginning the period of sacrifice with ashes of repentance, versus Valentine's Day, a day celebrating LOVE with fancy dinners and Valentine cards and gifts and special treats.

And yet, as I reflected on this convergence, it seemed rather appropriate! After all, the sacrifice of Jesus wasn't for His own sake, but was *an act of love* for others. And it started me thinking: what could I do for Lent that was a continuing, forty-day act of love toward others?

I decided to make *one phone call per day during Lent* to people in my life I hadn't spoken to in quite a while. Distant cousins, other extended family, former co-workers, distant friends, neighbors I hadn't seen in a while, former small group people, even some high school classmates. It took discipline! But, oh! What a blessing . . . to ME! (And yes, to the callee, as well.) To reach out and touch someone, tell them you care about them, catch up a little, remembering just how God blessed me by putting that person in my life. At times, the call seemed "God ordained"—just at the right time to encourage or pray with someone.

A sacrifice of love . . .

Something to try the next time Lent comes around?

Passover

Passover always comes in early spring (March or April). Passover is celebrated on the fourteenth day of the first month of the Hebrew calendar (Abib, later called Nisan).

Passover (*Pesach* in Hebrew) literally means "to pass over," a time to remember when the blood of a lamb on the doorposts saved the slaves in Egypt from the Angel of Death, who *passed over* that house when it saw the blood (see Exodus 6:6-8).

Passover is a time of beginnings for the Jewish people, celebrating the end of their slavery in Egypt and moving toward the Promised Land as God's people.

Two other festivals occur within days of each other: **The Feast of Unleavened Bread** and the **Feast of First Fruits.** In many cases, these three feasts are celebrated together and have become one.

Meaning for Christians

Jesus was celebrating the Passover meal the night He was betrayed and arrested. As He and His disciples ate together, He explained the symbolism of the various parts of the meal—the broken bread (His body), the wine poured out (His blood)—saving those who believe from the power of sin and death. (Also, the Feast of Unleavened Bread represents the burial of Jesus, and the Day of First Fruits, His resurrection.)

A Jewish Seder

The Passover meal and its rituals is called a "Seder." If you have an opportunity to attend a traditional Jewish Seder with a Jewish family or at a Jewish synagogue, by all means GO. Much of the *Haggadah* may be in Hebrew, but if you have a general idea of the various parts of the Seder meal (see "A Christian Seder" which follows), you'll get the idea. And feel free to ask questions! Your friendship and interest—even if you are a *goy*—will be appreciated.

But don't assume this is the time to point out all the Messianic implications of the Passover meal. However, if you have a Jewish friend with whom you feel free to discuss various points of Judaism and Christianity, it could be a very enlightening discussion! Start with how eagerly Jesus wanted to celebrate Passover with His disciples, and go from there . . .

Lashanan Habaÿah Bi Herusahlayim!
Next year in Jerusalem!

A Christian Seder

In *The Yada Yada Prayer Group Gets Rolling* (Book 6), the Yada Yada Prayer Group celebrates a Jewish Passover meal (a "Seder") with the Garfield family. This is one of the feasts commanded by the Lord in Leviticus 23:5-8, to commemorate God's deliverance from their bondage in Egypt.

For many Christians, the Jewish Passover meal has been relegated to Old Testament practices and has been replaced with a simple "Lord's Supper" or "Communion" or "Eucharist" (depending on your denominational affiliation)—primarily "drinking the cup" and "breaking the bread" which we do in remembrance of our Lord's shed blood and broken body. End of story.

But there are a growing number of Christian churches and families who have rediscovered the yearly Seder meal, with its rich traditions and—best of all—with its spiritual significance for us as Christians. So hold on to your Bible and let's take a fast journey backward through time . . .

Why Should We Celebrate Seder?

First, because it was important to Jesus. In the week leading up to His arrest and crucifixion, Jesus was *persona non grata* in Jerusalem. He had ridden into Jerusalem with all the people cheering, which upset the religious leaders no end. (Who did He think He was, anyway?) Then He strode into the Temple grounds and threw out the money changers and sacrificial animal vendors who were ripping off the people. Jesus then withdrew to Bethany to let things cool down a little, even while the religious leaders began plotting ways to get rid of Him.

So why did Jesus return to Jerusalem a few days later, when things were still so hot for Him? In Luke 22:15, Jesus tells His disciples, "With fervent desire I have desired to eat this Passover with you before I suffer" (NKJV). Jesus was eager to eat the yearly feast commanded by God in Leviticus, and sent His disciples ahead to prepare it.

Secondly, because Jesus told us to. During the Passover (Seder) meal, when it came time in the ritual to pour the cup of wine, and then to break the bread, Jesus gave deeper meaning to the symbolism of these events. As the Lamb of God, the cup symbolized *His* spilled blood. The broken bread, *His* body. Then He told His disciples, "Do this, whenever you drink it, do it in remembrance of me." (See I Corinthians 11:23-26, NIV)

The early Christians took this instruction seriously, and the Seder meal was celebrated with joyous wonder for the next three hundred years. Their eyes had been opened to its layers of significance, not only for what this feast symbolized regarding God's deliverance of His people in the past, but for how it pointed to the continuing work of God's salvation through the life, death, and resurrection of His Son, Jesus, delivering *all people* from the bondage of sin.

Certainly, we should continue to celebrate the "Lord's Supper" once a month (as many congregations do), or the "Eucharist" every Sunday (as liturgical churches do), but why not *also* celebrate that rich prophetic Seder meal once a year, along with Jesus and His disciples?

Preparing for Your Seder Meal

Invite guests! Especially guests with children or teens. The purpose of the Seder meal is to invite questions from children.

Set the table for a festive meal—a tablecloth, flowers, candles (important), and your best dishes. (If you've invited more people than you have dishes, and have to use paper goods, use colorful paper plates or Chinet.)

Set the table for one more than the number of guests expected (if possible)—this is for Elijah.

Each place setting should have a wine goblet or glass.

A bowl for hand washing, along with a small towel, should be placed near the head of the table or nearby.

Place a *Haggadah* (the Order of Service) at each place setting, or every other place so guests can share. (See the **Resources** on page 19 to obtain copies of a Christian Haggadah. You will want to decide whether to use a "long version" or a "shortened version." The online versions can be printed out and photocopied for your guests.)

Optional: You might want to put a pillow or cushion on each chair for leaning on, in the spirit of the **Four Questions** (see pages 18 and 19).

The Seder Plate

Near the head of the table, place a fancy serving plate with the following symbolic items:

- **A shank bone of a lamb**—which represents the lamb that was slain to obtain blood to put on the doorposts of every Israelite home.
- **Bitter herbs** (grated horseradish)—representing the bitterness of life for the Israelites as slaves in Egypt
- ***Karpas*** (a green vegetable, usually parsley, good for dipping in the salt water)—the salt water represents the tears shed while the Israelites were in bondage
- ***Charoset*** (a mixture of chopped apples, chopped nuts, moistened with wine or grape juice)—represents the mortar they had to make to hold bricks together
- Three pieces of ***matzo***, wrapped within a cloth napkin—for the Christian, represents the unity of One God: Father, Son, and Holy Spirit.

What Else Goes on the Table

Place several of the following on the table within everyone's reach:

- Small bowls of salty water.
- Enough parsley sprigs so each person can have one.
- A plate of matzo (unleavened crackers, available in your grocery store).
- A bottle of wine or grape juice (for every four to six people, if you pour only "symbolic" amounts).
- Extra serving bowls of the bitter herbs (horseradish) and the *charoset* (apples/nuts/wine mixture).

What Happens During a Seder (General)

When your guests arrive, seat them at the table, and give each one the *Haggadah,* or Order of Service. (The *Haggadah* for a Christian Seder will highlight the Messianic "foretellings" which were fulfilled in Jesus the Messiah.) Tell your guests that even though you are going to follow the Order of Service, it's all right to interrupt and ask questions.

The mother or hostess **lights the candles** with a blessing.

The father or leader **washes his hands.** (But when Jesus celebrated the Passover, He washed the *feet* of His disciples! Some churches include footwashing with a simple meal on "Maundy Thursday" before Good Friday.)

The youngest child (or four children) asks the traditional **Four Questions**, which the leader answers, explaining the meaning of the symbolic items on the Seder Plate and why things are done a certain way.

The leader **retells the story of the escape from Egypt from Exodus 12**. (Read the story ahead of time so you can tell it in dramatic fashion.)

Your story might also include a summary of the **Ten Plagues** God sent as judgment of Egypt for not letting His people go. As each plague is mentioned, each person can dip a finger into their cup of wine or grape juice, and flick a drop onto their plate: (1) Blood! . . . (2) Frogs! . . . (3) Lice! . . . (4) Flies! . . . (5) Livestock disease! . . . (6) Boils! . . . (7) Hail! . . . (8) Locusts! . . . (9) Darkness! . . . (10) Death of the firstborn!

Eat bitter herbs (horseradish) with a small amount of *charoset* on the matzo crackers.

The leader unwraps the three matzo and breaks the middle one in two. He wraps one of the broken pieces in a separate cloth, then hides it for the children to find later. This is called the ***Afikomen***. (The broken middle matzo represents the broken body of Christ, which was buried—hidden—until God raised Him from the dead.)

Throughout the service, four glasses of wine are poured and drunk, each with its own blessing. Since this is symbolic, you might want to pour just a little bit of wine or grape juice in each glass—at least until the actual meal!

Eat the festive meal! This might include Matzo Ball Soup (see page 130); chicken or lamb; potato kugel; gefilte fish (a delicacy—not!); etc.

After the meal, the third and fourth cups of wine are poured and blessed. The door is opened for the prophet Elijah.

The children hunt for the ***Afikomen***. The child who finds it can ransom it for a price (which means the leader has to dig in his pockets for a few coins!)—just as Jesus paid our ransom price.

At the end of the Seder meal and service, everyone says: **"Next year in Jerusalem!"** (Expressing, for many displaced Jews, the hope that one day they would celebrate Passover in Jerusalem once again. For Christians, we look forward to a New Jerusalem, where we will live with Christ forever.)

The Four Questions

It is important for children to be included in the Seder celebration. During the service and before the meal, the youngest child (or four different children) asks the following questions, which are answered by the leader of the table:

Q. 1—On all other nights we eat all kinds of breads and crackers. **Why do we eat only matzo at Passover?**
A. 1—Matzo reminds us that when the Children of Israel left Egypt, they had no time to bake bread. They took along raw dough and baked it on hot rocks in the desert—represented by the matzo we eat today.

Q. 2—On all other nights we eat many kinds of vegetables and herbs. **Why do we eat bit-**

ter herbs at our Seder meal?

A. 2—The bitter herbs remind us of the bitter and cruel way King Pharoah treated the Israelite slaves in Egypt.

Q. 3—On all other nights we don't usually dip our food, but at our Seder meal we dip parsley in the salt water, and the bitter herbs in the *Charoset.* **Why do we dip our foods twice tonight?**

A. 3—We dip bitter herbs into the *Charoset* to remind us how hard the Israelite people worked to make bricks for Pharoah's buildings.

Q. 4—On all other nights we eat sitting up straight. **Why do we lean on a pillow tonight?**

A. 4—Tonight we lean on a pillow as a reminder that once we were slaves, but now we are free!

Resources for Your Seder

A 24-page reproducible Haggadah from a Messianic perspective is included in the book, *A Family Guide to the Biblical Holidays* by Robin Sampson and Linda Pierce (Heart of Wisdom Publishers). Available online at www.biblicalholidays.com, www.amazon.com, and other sources.

More ideas from the above book for celebrating Seder can be found at www.biblicalholidays.com.

"The Passover Seder for Christians," an *Haggadah* adapted by Dennis Bratcher, is available at www.crivoice.org/haggadah.html. You may download and photocopy this Seder service for no charge (with certain restrictions). Includes responsive readings, blessings, prayers, etc. More information and ideas—including ideas for celebrating Seder with a large church group or celebrating only a *symbolic* Seder—can be found on the same site at: www.crivoice.org/seder.html.

Juneteenth

Never heard of Juneteenth? Not surprising. "Juneteenth" is a *portmanteau,* a blending of the words "June" and "Nineteenth," the day in 1865 when black slaves in Texas finally got the word that they were free—two and a half years *after* the Emancipation Proclamation.

Ironic. A little-known holiday about an event that is little known. And yet incredibly significant for African Americans and their history in this country.

A little background

In an attempt to squeeze out more unpaid work cultivating their cotton crops and running their large plantations, slave owners in Texas deliberately withheld the news that all slaves in the United States of America had been proclaimed "free" on January 1, 1863, the date the Emancipation Proclamation went into effect. Finally, the U.S. government sent the military to enforce the Proclamation. Arriving in Galveston, Texas, with a contingent of soldiers, Major General Gordon Granger made three pronouncements, called General Orders:

> **General Order #3** declared that "all slaves are free."
> **General Order #4** required that all civil and military personnel connected to "the Confederate State" must report for parole and all of their acts and laws were now illegitimate.
> **General Order #5** stated that all cotton grown by free (unpaid) labor [since the Emancipation Proclamation] had to be shipped to New York or New Orleans by the plantation owners.

Suddenly thrust into freedom, former slaves now had to choose:

- They could stay with their former slave owners, who were now obligated to pay them wages as employees.
- They could go in search of family members who had been sold away into slavery and try to reestablish their family unit.
- They could set out on this unknown journey called "freedom," in spite of incredible odds, and make of it what they could.

Tough choices. Freedom came hard, as we all know. Freed men and women faced discrimination, economic and educational disparities, the Ku Klux Klan, segregation, harassment and prejudice for many decades to come.

But those who celebrate Juneteenth are celebrating *the freedom to choose.*

Acknowledging the Day

Ironically, Texas was the first to declare "Juneteenth" a state holiday in 1980! Since then, 45 other states have established "Juneteenth" as a state holiday or a special day of observance. The National Juneteenth Observance Foundation (www.nationaljuneteenth.com) is urging the U.S. government to make it a national holiday/observance.

Still, Juneteenth is usually an unsung holiday. As often as not, June 19 passes with little recognition for many of us, even in many African American communities.

We could change that, you know. Because if "we're not free until all of us are free," then celebrating a major milestone of freedom for any of our brothers and sisters is appropriate for all of us!

So, Let's Celebrate!

First, find out if there are any Juneteenth observances in your local area. If open to the public, join in!

Or, create your own:

For African American families, Juneteenth is an appropriate time for a family reunion (see pages 20 and 64). After all, *family* is the cornerstone of the African American community.

If you're not up for a big shebang that brings relatives from all over, then a family-and-friends barbeque on June 19 in the backyard or at a local park is a great opportunity to educate the young and celebrate this important day.

If you're not African American, but have African American friends, acquaintances, church members, neighbors, or co-workers, tell them you'd like to help celebrate this important day and "what can I bring?"

Food. For many, traditional food would include: barbecued beef or pork; smothered chicken; collard greens; black-eyed peas; red rice; cornbread; peach cobbler; red velvet cake; strawberry soda; sweet tea. (Why red soda? A drink forbidden to them as slaves, it was the first drink freed men and women celebrated with. Other red foods—red rice, red velvet cake, hibiscus tea, watermelon, strawberry pie—also joined the celebration, representing the blood spilled during slavery.)

Music. Choose favorite songs that speak of freedom and represent the souls of black folks. Also, spirituals and gospel music that honor your faith journey.

Dance. Might as well. Can't help it!

Read . . . the Emancipation Proclamation (find it online and print it out for everyone to read together in one voice) *and* General Orders #3, which says:

> The people of Texas are informed that, in accordance with a proclamation from the Executive of the United

States, "all slaves are free." This involves an absolute equality of personal rights and rights of property between former masters and slaves, and the connection heretofore existing between them becomes that between employer and hired labor. The freedmen are advised to remain quietly at their present homes and work for wages. They are informed that they will not be allowed to collect at military posts, and that they will not be supported in idleness either there or elsewhere.

—By command of Maj. Gen. Granger
June 19, 1865

One Last Thing—Making the Day Count

Beverly Sanders, a librarian in Valdosta, Georgia, had never heard of Juneteenth growing up. But when she did hear about it, she used the observance as a chance to educate her neighborhood youth and do a fundraiser to build up the local library in the Black neighborhood, which had lots of bare shelves and no budget for new books. A three-day celebration around Juneteenth featured special programs at the library, a free barbecue, and a fundraising dinner which netted $30,000 for the library.

Just wondering . . . what worthwhile project around Juneteenth could benefit African American youth in *your* community?

Fourth of July

What more can we say about the Fourth of July, our national Independence Day? Most schools, towns, cities, communities, and states have this holiday already well-covered—from New York City to tiny Lambert, Montana. (Shout out to my ancestral small town and relations who are the backbone of that farming community!) No matter where you live, you don't have to go far to find parades, picnics, backyard BBQs, fireworks . . . For families, it's the most fun summer holiday of the year. So, go ahead! Celebrate in the manner to which you are accustomed!

But here are a few thoughts to keep in mind:

(1) Not everyone was given freedom or equality with the Declaration of Independence in 1776. Slavery in this country would continue for another 87 years until the Emancipation Proclamation. Women could not vote until 1920—144 years later. Freedom is a work in progress. We can't take our freedoms for granted. We need to protect them for *everyone.*

(2) None of us are truly free until everyone is free. Many people groups in this country have had to march, protest, and demand their civil rights in order to experience equal treatment under the law.

(3) The U.S. Congress has enacted not one,

not two, but *six* Civil Rights Acts to hopefully grant the same liberties to all persons living in this country:

- The **Civil Rights Act of 1866** declared all persons born in the United States were now citizens, without regard to race, color, or previous condition.
- The **Civil Rights Act of 1875** was enacted during Reconstruction in response to civil rights violations to African Americans "to protect all citizens in their civil and legal rights." *Unfortunately,* this Act was declared unconstitutional by the Supreme Court in 1883 during Civil Rights cases, paving the way for the future of segregation and discrimination well into the 1950s.
- The **Civil Rights Act of 1957** empowered federal prosecutors to obtain court injunctions against interference with the right to vote.
- The **Civil Rights Act of 1964**, one of the most important civil rights legislations, ended segregation in public places and banned employment discrimination on the basis of race, color, religion, sex, or national origin.
- The **Civil Rights Act of 1965** outlawed discriminatory voting practices adopted in many southern states after the Civil War.
- The **Civil Rights Act of 1968** is commonly called the Fair Housing Act of 1968, outlawing housing discrimination, defined as the "refusal to sell or rent a dwelling to any person because of his race, color, religion, or national origin."

This year, why not read the full text of the **Declaration of Independence** together as a family? Easily found online. At the very least, everyone should be able to quote these precious lines:

> We hold these truths to be self-evident, that all [men and women] are created equal, that they are endowed by their Creator with certain unalienable Rights, that among these are Life, Liberty, and the pursuit of Happiness.

Rosh Hashanah
The Jewish New Year

Rosh Hashanah comes in the early fall, September or October. (The first day of Tishri, the seventh month on the Jewish calendar.)

Also known as the Feast of Trumpets, i.e. the blowing of the shofar marks the beginning of this festival. (See Numbers 29:1-6; Leviticus. 23:23-25.)

Rosh Hashanah marks the beginning of the Ten Days of Awe (between Rosh Hashanah and Yom Kippur), a time of introspection—a spiritual inventory, as it were, to prepare one's heart for the coming of the Messiah.

Background

Read Nehemiah 8 (especially verses 9 and 10): "Then Nehemiah the governor, Ezra the priest and teacher of the Law, and the Levites who were instructing the people said to them all, 'This day is holy to the Lord your God. Do not mourn or weep.' For all the people had been weeping as they listened to the words of the Law. Nehemiah said, 'Go and enjoy choice food and sweet drinks, and send some to those who have nothing prepared. This day is holy to our Lord. Do not grieve, for the joy of the Lord is your strength'" (NIV).

Meaning for Christians

Preparing our hearts with expectancy for Yeshua's second coming, which will be announced by the blowing of a trumpet (Matthew 24:31; 1 Corinthians 15:52; 1 Thessalonians 4:16-17).

Ways to Celebrate

Take time to do a "spiritual inventory," both personally and as a family. Have you been letting your personal Bible reading or prayer times get swallowed up by busyness? Have you been meaning to have family Bible reading and prayer but just haven't gotten around to it? Early fall (the beginning of a new school year for kids) is a good time to reevaluate your family schedule and priorities.

Attend Rosh Hashanah services at a nearby Messianic congregation or Jewish synagogue.

Ask a Jewish friend to come to dinner and share with your family what Rosh Hashanah means to them.

Traditional Foods for Rosh Hashanah (and Their Meanings):

Challah bread: The round shape symbolizes a perfect year to come. Sometimes raisins or honey are added to make it extra sweet.

Apples and honey: Apples slices are dipped in honey to symbolize a wish for a sweet year to come.

Gefilte ("filled") fish: Fish symbolizes fruitfulness, fertility, and abundance. The fish head symbolizes the head (start) of the New Year, and the desire to lead other nations by living in a just and upright manner.

Tzimmes (honey baked carrots): From the Yiddish word *"meren"* (which means "carrots" and "to increase"), symbolizing the desire to increase one's good deeds in the coming year. (Some Eastern European *tzimmes* recipes add prunes, sweet potatoes, or even meat to the sweet carrots for a "sweet entree.")

Spinach: Symbolizes a green year with plenty of produce.

Rice: Also symbolizes abundance.

Honey Cake or Teiglach (crunchy dough boiled in honey): And once more, "Have a sweet New Year!"

Yom Kippur
Day of Atonement

Yom Kippur falls ten days after Rosh Hashanah, concluding the Ten Days of Awe. (The tenth day of Tishri.)

Yom Kippur is a fast day, not a feast day—a day of confession, repentance, and cleansing, when God made a way through the priests and animal sacrifices to atone for the sins of the people. (See Numbers 29:7-11; Leviticus 23:26-32.)

Meaning for Christians

Jesus has already made atonement for our sins on the cross (see Romans 3:23-26). With grateful hearts we look forward to that great day when the Book of Life in which our names appear will be opened and read.

Ways to Celebrate

Talk together as a family about fasting, its purpose (setting aside a special time for prayer and renewal), and the various kinds of fasts (e.g., the "Daniel Fast," which is eating only vegetables and drinking only water). Choose an appropriate "fast" for your family—skipping one meal, fasting from certain foods or entertainment, or etc.

This may be a good time to review with your family what "atonement" means, and the fact that God sent His Son Jesus to offer His life as a sacrifice and pay the penalty for our sins. Parents, be alert—one or more of your children may want to ask Jesus to write his or her name in the Book of Life on this day!

More ideas can be found at www.biblical-holidays.com.

Books for your bookshelf: *A Family Guide to the Biblical Holidays* by Robin Sampson and Linda Pierce (Heart of Wisdom Publishers). Also recommended: *The Fall Feasts of Israel* by Mitch Glaser and Zhava Glaser (Moody Press, 1987). Written from a Messianic perspective.

Sukkot
The Feast of Booths

If Ruth Garfield, the Yada Yada sister who is a Messianic Jew, wasn't so distracted being pregnant with twins, she'd want to tell you about Sukkot, the most joyous of the Fall festivals celebrated by the Jewish people.

Background

Also known as the Feast of Booths or the Feast of Tabernacles (or Shelters)—also spelled *Succoth* or *Sukkoth* and pronounced "sue-*coat*"—Sukkot is a seven-day festival in memory of the time the Children of Israel lived in tents in the wilderness, a time of thanksgiving for God's care and provision. (See Numbers 29:12-38; Leviticus 23:33-35; 39-43, especially verse 42.)

The Feast of Booths in the Old Testament

Sukkot begins five days after Yom Kippur, the Day of Atonement, on the fifteenth day of Tishri on the Jewish calendar (usually September or October). It is variously called The Feast of Booths, The Feast of Tabernacles, or Sukkot (which is the plural of *sukkah,* which means "booth" or "shelter").

This festival was commanded by the Lord in Leviticus 23:33-43 as a time to remember God's care and provision when the Israelite people lived in temporary dwellings out in the desert, before they came into the Promised Land.

> The Lord said to Moses, "Say to the Israelites: 'On the fifteenth day of the seventh month the Lord's Feast of Tabernacles [Shelters] begins . . . after you have gathered the crops of the land, celebrate the festival to the Lord for seven days; the first day is a day of rest, and the eighth day also is a day of rest. . . . Live in booths for seven days . . . so your descendants will know that I had the Israelites live in booths when I brought them out of Egypt. I am the Lord your God'" (NIV).

The celebration itself was fairly simple: build temporary shelters; live in them; invite others to share meals with you in the shelter; give thanks to God for His bountiful harvest; and the first day and the day after the festival (the eighth day) were to be days of rest.

Only one specific ritual is associated with the Feast of Booths. God instructed Moses, "On the first day, gather *fruit from citrus trees*, and collect *palm fronds* and other *leafy branches* and *willows* that grow by the streams. Then rejoice before the Lord your God for seven days" (Leviticus 23:40, NLT, emphasis added). According to Jewish tradition, these plants are called the Four

Species. The leafy branches—palm fronds, willow, myrtle (reeds may be substituted)—are bound together and called the *lulav*, which are waved around the booth at various times during the seven days. The *citron fruit* (e.g. oranges or other citrus) are used to help decorate the booth, along with gourds, squash, and other vegetables and fruits readily available during this harvest time.

The seventh day is called *Hashannah Rabbah*, and is often the first day of rain after the harvest. The booth is then taken down, and the eighth day (called *Shmenie Atzeret*) is a day of rest.

The purpose of this festival is to remember that God took care of His people, even when they were living in temporary shelters, even before they entered into the Promised Land. (It is also significant to notice that *God Himself* also dwelt in a temporary Tabernacle during this time, before the Temple in Jerusalem was built.)

The Feast of Booths in the New Testament

Did you know that Jesus observed the Feast of Booths? He taught in the temple during this festival, and the many pilgrims who had come to Jerusalem for the feast heard Him speak. You can read about it in John 7:10 ff. Notice especially verses 37-39 (NIV):

> On the last and greatest day of the Feast, Jesus stood and said in a loud voice, "If anyone is thirsty, let him come to me and drink. Whoever believes in me, as the Scripture has said, streams of living water will flow from within him." By this he meant the Spirit, whom those who believed in him were later to receive. Up to that time the Spirit had not been given, since Jesus had not yet been glorified.

This happened on *Hashannah Rabbah*, the day associated with the fall rains! What a beautiful reminder that all the Jewish feasts point to and are fulfilled in the coming of the Messiah.

Spiritual Meanings of this Festival . . . and it's significance for us today.

God is our shelter. In our materialistic society, it's so easy to take for granted the blessings of our homes, cars, dishwashers, and telephones. Living in a temporary shelter (even if only for a few hours, or sleeping in it overnight) can help us focus our thoughts on the One who is our shelter, whether we are rich or poor. As Paul the Apostle said, "I have learned the secret of being content in any and every situation, whether well fed or hungry, whether living in plenty or in want. I can do everything through him who gives me strength" (Philippians 4:12b, 13, NIV).

This world is not our home. As the children's chorus goes, "This world is not my home, I'm just a-passing through . . ."

Building a *sukkah* and spending some time in it can help remind us just how temporary this life is. Meanwhile, Jesus is preparing a glorious eternal home for us in heaven! (Read John 14:1-4.)

We don't have to live in bondage to sin. Just as God brought out the Children of Israel from bondage in Egypt when they applied "the blood of a lamb" on their doorposts, so Jesus has freed us from the bondage of sin by offering Himself as the Lamb of God, the ultimate sacrifice for our sin. Our journey with Jesus may not yet feel like we've reached the "promised land," but we are *free.*

The "last great day." The seventh day of this festival was often referred to as the "last great day of the feast." As such, it prophetically points toward that Last Great Day when God's people will dwell with Him forever. *Read John 7:37-39 again.* It was on the "last and greatest day of the feast" that Jesus invited those who were "thirsty for God" to come to Him and "drink," and "streams of living water" would flow from within them—a reference to the gift of the Holy Spirit when Jesus returned to heaven, and also to that Last Great Day when Jesus will come again.

Suggestions for Celebrating Sukkot

Build a sukkah! No, we're not going to go into construction details here. (Google "Feast of Booths" or "Building a Sukkah" and you will probably find a variety of instructions on the Internet. Also see Resources below.) But the general idea is to build a temporary structure in your yard, made of natural materials if possible. You can use scrap lumber, covered by branches, or even sheets. However, some families pitch a tent and "sleep out" during Sukkot. The whole point is not to get hung up on the details, but to experience a temporary dwelling in some way during this seven-day festival, and create special memories as a family. (One family with sick children made a tent with sheets in their living room, in which they ate and slept.)

Decorate your sukkah. Use branches, gourds, pumpkins, fruit—anything to reflect the joy of harvest. According to tradition, the lamps burning in the sukkahs during this festival lit up the whole city. Use strings of lights as part of your decoration.

Spend time in your sukkah. Use it for your time alone with God, reflecting on some of the spiritual themes of this festival (see above). Eat as many meals as possible in your temporary dwelling. If possible, sleep in your sukkah at least one night, looking at the stars through your very temporary roof!

Invite guests to celebrate with you. Sukkot is also a harvest festival, a time to thank God for His abundant provision. This is a feast! Invite a neighbor family; a single coworker; a newcomer to your church. Rejoice! Eat, drink, and be merry! (And why not invite a Jewish friend to eat with you and explain this tradition to your family?)

Read Scriptures that explain the Feast of Tabernacles. See Leviticus 23:34-43; Deuteronomy 16:13-15; and Numbers 29:12-40.

Read the Bible story about Jesus and the Feast of Tabernacles. See John 7:2-39.

Wave the lulav. Bind together the different kinds of branches mentioned in Leviticus 23:40, and let your children wave them as you sing songs of praise after one of your festive meals in the sukkah.

Suggested Resources

More ideas can be found at www.biblical-holidays.com.

Books for your bookshelf: *A Family Guide to the Biblical Holidays* by Robin Sampson and Linda Pierce (Heart of Wisdom Publishers). Also recommended: *The Fall Feasts of Israel* by Mitch Glaser and Zhava Glaser (Moody Press, 1987). Written from a Messianic perspective.

Now, as Ruth Garfield would say, "You're waiting for what? The sky to fall? Go build yourself a *sukkah*. A lot of fun you will have!"

Mexican Independence Day Fiesta

Did you know . . . Latino Americans are now the largest minority group in the United States? All major cities and many other communities North, South, East, and West have significant Latino populations. Translated into Yada Yada terms, that means there are probably Spanish-speaking mothers and fathers, babies and teenagers, aunts and uncles and grandparents in most neighborhoods who shop at the grocery store, attend local schools, work around town, and attend Bible-believing churches. We are an immigrant nation, and *these* immigrants—some of whom have been U.S. citizens for generations—bring a rich heritage to America's quilt-of-many-colors.

Latino or Hispanic?

Yikes! Which word do we use for characters in the Yada Yada Prayer Group novels? Is Edesa Reyes *Latina*? Is Delores Enriquez *Hispanic*? We discovered the jury's still out about which is the preferred word, even among Spanish-speaking Americans. "Hispanic" has often been used to refer to those from Mexico, Puerto Rico, and Cuba, as well as Spain ("*Hispania*"), whereas "Latino" refers to a broad spectrum with Latin American heritage (both Spanish and Portuguese–speaking).

But that's not necessarily how Spanish-speaking people identify themselves. Some prefer "Latino" regardless of country of origin because it arises from the Spanish-speaking community itself, whereas "Hispanic" is the official word used by the United States government on census records, etc. However, a recent poll revealed another surprising result: The term "Hispanic" was preferred by a majority of second and third generation citizens who tend to be more assimilated, whereas "Latino" was preferred by the older generation, who still tend to view the term "Hispanic" as colonialistic.

Another slight difference: "Hispanic" is an adjective, whereas "Latino" can be either a noun or adjective. Also, "Latino" or "Latina" can be used to specify gender.

In the Yada Yada novels, we had to make a judgment call and chose "Latino" both because it is self-identifying, and also because it can be gender specific. But whether *Latino* or *Hispanic*, we value and celebrate our Spanish-speaking brothers and sisters! Which is why we encourage readers to . . .

Time of Year: September 16

September 16 is a major holiday, not only in Mexico, but in Mexican-American communities all over the United States (just as Irish Americans celebrate St. Patrick's Day with all its Irish traditions). On this date in 1810, Father Miguel Hidalgo rang the church bell in the town of Dolores to gather the townspeople, and issued a cry for independence from three centuries of Spanish rule: *"Mexicanos, ¡Viva México!"* ("Mexicans! Long live Mexico!"). Thus began a ten-year struggle for independence, which was finally granted by the Spanish viceroy in 1821.

(***NOTE:*** Mexico's independence is often confused with Cinco de Mayo (the Fifth of May), but that fiesta commemorates the Battle of Puebla between Mexican and French forces in 1862. However, both holidays are opportunities to celebrate Mexican heritage and colorful culture.)

It's easy to know when September arrives in Chicago where the Yada Yadas live. Huge green, white, and red flags fly from cars all week long as horns honk and street vendors do a brisk business of roasted ears of Mexican corn, cheese nachos, *chicharrones* (pork rinds), tamales, and *champurrado* (thick hot chocolate flavored with cinnamon). The high point for many is the downtown parade along Columbus Drive with its colorful floats, folk dancers, mariachi bands, and more—not to mention the popular neighborhood parades.

But whether or not your town celebrates Mexico's Independence Day, this Fiesta is a great time to get better acquainted with your Mexican-American neighbors. Here are a few ways to join the celebration!

Brush Up on Your History

A trip to the library or an online search on Mexico should yield some family-friendly background on our closest neighbor south of the border. During the week of September 16, announce ahead of time that all family members need to tell something new they've learned about Mexico as their "ticket" to supper on the chosen night.

Watch *The Mission,* a 1986 British film (rated PG—some scenes may be disturbing to young children) that tells the story of Father Gabriel, a Jesuit priest who treks deep into the heart of a South American rainforest to build a peaceful Christian mission among the Guarani Indians in the eighteenth century. But aggressive Portuguese slave traders thwart his mission and lead to tragedy. While this film is not about Mexico, it represents the struggle of the colonial years in South America.

Invite a Mexican-American acquaintance, friend, or family to your home to share his or her own history. (This could be part of your own Backyard Fiesta—see below!)

Get in on the Fun

How is Mexican Independence Day celebrated in *your* community? Choose from the following:

(1) Take the family to a Mexican Independence Day Parade.

(2) Take the family to a public fiesta (dancing! music! food!) in a local park.

(3) Take the family to an authentic Mexican restaurant (preferably one with a mariachi band!) and enjoy traditional dishes such as Mole Poblano, Chiles en Nogada, guacamole and chips, and much more!

Or . . . Host Your Own Backyard Fiesta!

(Or if your backyard isn't suitable, make it a Block Party! Many cities allow a neighborhood to sign up for a Block Party, and the police will even bring street barriers to keep traffic at bay so the kids can ride their bikes, trikes, and roller skates in the street while the adults haul out the tables and lawn chairs.)

- **Who to invite?** The neighbors, of course! Or your extended family! Or folks from church! But do your best to include some Mexican American families from school, church, or work—and ask for their suggestions on how to create a fiesta for *gringos.*
- **How to decorate?** Small green, white, and red Mexican flags of course—as well as the good ol' red, white, and blue! Use green, white, and red as your color scheme—or just bright, vibrant colors in general (no pastels here!). Use crepe paper or mini-lights wound around trees, bushes, porch railings—whatever works in your back yard.
- **What to eat?** Make it potluck, but ask ev-

eryone to bring something "south of the border": chips and salsa, tortillas, taco makings, enchiladas (page 89), burritos, Spanish rice, refried beans, quesadillas, *carnitas* (page 97), *pan de polvo* (page 93)—the possibilities are endless.

- **Music, of course!** A live band would be awesome—but most of us might have to settle for a CD player and your favorite Mexican music: *mariachi* (guitars, violins, trumpets); *banda* (brass); *norteño* (accordion and guitars), Mexican *cumbia* (drums, congas, accordion, bass guitar), or some of your favorite popular Spanish artists. (You can check out CDs from your local library if you don't have any on hand.)
- **And for the kids . . .** a piñata, of course! They aren't very expensive and are loads of fun. Hang the piñata from the limb of a tree (or other creative substitute!) just above head level, with plenty of clear space around it. You will need a blindfold and a plastic bat. Let the little ones try first (they get three tries); then the bigger children (two tries?). Keep all children except for the "batter" out of reach of the swinging bat. When the piñata breaks, there is usually a mad scramble for the rain of candy, of course. (Be careful that the "batter" quits swinging before other kids dive into harm's way!) One way to insure all kids get a fair share is to have everyone dump the candy they pick up into a large bowl. Then divvy it out in little plastic bags.
- **But most of all,** enjoy getting to know real people who represent one of the many cultures that make up the *United* States of America. Mexican Americans are our neighbors—in more ways than one.

Hallelujah Fest (Halloween Alternative)

When Jodi Baxter was growing up, Halloween was just a time to carve grinning Jack-o-lanterns out of big orange pumpkins, dress up in costumes (everything from princesses, super heroes, sheet-wearing ghosts, and cowboys), and to trek from house to house throughout the neighborhood yelling, "Trick or treat!" All innocent fun.

But there's a dark side to Halloween. Haunted houses. Eggs thrown at windows. Mean tricks for those who don't dish out the candy. Slasher movies full of terror and gore in the theaters and on TV.

Ever wonder where the term "Halloween" came from? On the church calendar, November 1 is All Saints Day, a day to honor the saints who have died and gone to heaven. Therefore, the evening *before* All Saints Day, October 31, was called "All Hallows Eve" or

"Hallow (Holy) E'en" (evening). For many, this was a holy day, remembering saints of old. But for others, it marked a pagan "celebration of the dead," a dark and sinister time full of ghosts, ghouls, and witches' spells.

What to do? After all, kids love to parade around in costumes! You *could* ban Halloween altogether. Or you could encourage an alternative, a . . .

Hallelujah Fest!

Or call it a "Harvest Festival." Or a "Festival of Light." Any of these themes would be appropriate for the time of year. The benefits are enormous.

Many parents would welcome a Halloween alternative that would be fun, yet keep their kids off the street at night.

An opportunity for your church to invite kids and parents from the neighborhood for a party.

Compared to simple trick or treating, a Hallelujah Fest has the potential to be lots more fun—complete with costumes and candy, too!

Invitations

Make up a simple flyer at least two weeks before October 31 with all pertinent information and make sure it goes home with all the families in your church. Pass out the flyers in the neighborhood surrounding your church, too—or encourage families to bring another family from their own neighborhood. Besides *date, time,* and *place,* the flyer should include:

All children must be accompanied by an adult.

Encourage all children *and* adults to come in costume (see **Costume Ideas**, below). Pick a costume theme, or simply encourage non-scary costumes.

What Each Family Should Bring:

This depends on your plans for your festival! But it might include: A roll of cheap toilet paper (for the "Mummy Wrap"); a bag of candy (to mix and hand out to the kids in goodie bags); nonperishable food (cans, packages, or boxes) if you are collecting for a food pantry; a candle in a jar or a lantern, if you go caroling in the neighborhood; and/or etc.

Costume Ideas

- Avoid ghoulish or violent costumes.
- Pick a theme: Fairy Tale characters; Biblical characters; animal characters; or etc.
- Encourage "family group" costumes, or "pairs" and "sets": E.g., Raggedy Ann and Andy; Flopsy, Mopsy, and Cottontail; R2 D2 and C-3PO; The Three Bears; Little Red Riding Hood and the Wolf; Luke Skywalker and Princess Leia; Mary and Joseph; David and Goliath; etc.
- During your Festival, have a Costume Parade! You could have prizes for Most Original, Best Family Group, Funniest, etc.

Games

Mummy Wrap. Using the roll of toilet paper each family brought, each set of kids have to wrap their "mummy" (mommy) with a roll of T.P. First family to use up the whole role wins the prize! (*Note:* To make sure all the rolls of T.P. are the same size, you may have to provide the toilet paper.)

Relays! There are dozens to choose from, such as: (1) ***Cotton Ball Carry***—team members carry a cotton ball in a spoon around a marker and back again (harder than it sounds!); (2) ***Pass the Orange*** under the chin from person to person (if it drops, the orange has to go back two people); (3) ***Lifesaver Relay***—pass out toothpicks to team members, then each team has to pass a Lifesaver from toothpick to toothpick *held in the teeth* (no hands!); first team to finish first wins.

Bucket Toss. Divide into teams. You will need a bucket and an ordinary 1-pound bag of dry beans per team. Mark off toe lines with masking tape: 3 feet from bucket for little ones; 4-5 feet from bucket for older kids; 5-6 feet from bucket for teens and adults. Idea is to toss beans into the bucket! Team with highest score wins!

Refreshments

Keep it simple! Plates of cookies, fresh veggies, fruit slices, and cold (or hot) apple cider will help offset the little goodie bags of candy that will go home with each child. (Collect the bags of candy as each family arrives, mix it all together, then ask a couple volunteers to create little goodie bags for the kids to take home. Plastic sandwich bags tied with ribbon will do the trick.)

Story Time

Ask a good storyteller to tell the story of one or more great Christian heroes of the faith. A good resource is *Hero Tales: A Family Treasury of True Stories From the Lives of Christian Heroes, Vols. I-IV,* plus *Heroes in Black History*, all by Dave and Neta Jackson (Bethany House).

Or . . . several adults could dress up in costume as various Christian heroes and tell "their" story in dramatic first-person. The list is endless, but here are some possibilities:

Amy Carmichael, missionary to India;
Dwight Moody, from shoe salesman to evangelist;
Harriet Tubman, conductor on the Underground Railroad;
William and Catherine Booth, founders of the Salvation Army;
Eric Liddell, Olympic champion;

Florence Nightingale, army nurse;
Jim Elliot, a modern martyr,
. . . and many more.

Sing Songs of Light!

Make up a song sheet, or simply sing songs most will know. E.g., "This Little Light of Mine"; "When the Saints Go Marching In"; "I Want to Walk as a Child of the Light"; "Jesus is the Light of the World, Alleluia"; "Sing Hosanna (Give me oil in my lamp, keep me burning)"; "Hold Out Your Light, You Heaven-Bound Pilgrim"; etc.

Shine your light in the neighborhood! Help everyone light the candles they brought in jars and take your songs of praise to the streets.

Add Your Own Ideas . . .

These ideas for an "alternative Halloween" are just for starters. But there's one guarantee: all who attend will be clamoring to do it again next year. ("Mo-om! We *always* do a Hallelujah Fest on Halloween!") And thus a tradition begins.

Celebrate Thanksgiving

Thanksgiving! *Giving thanks* . . . that's what this holiday is about. Families getting together. And food, of course. Lots and lots of food. Most every family has their favorite foods and recipes, from the traditional turkey (*and* ham *and* macaroni and cheese, staples at most African-American Thanksgiving tables) to pumpkin pie (or sweet potato pie,). But before you dive in, it's worth taking a few minutes to reflect on the historical aspects of this day.

Reflect

The following account of the "First Thanksgiving" in the New World provides a meaningful context. However, the Native American corn mentioned here was not popcorn, nor would it have been very suitable for eating on the cob. It was primarily ground for meal.

> Our [wheat] did prove well, and God be praised, we had a good increase of Indian corn, and our barley indifferent good, but our peas not worth the gathering, for we feared they were too late sown. They came up very well, and blossomed, but the sun parched them in the blossom. Our harvest being gotten in, our governor sent four

> men [out] fowling, . . . so we might . . . rejoice together after we had gathered the fruit of our labors.
>
> They . . . in one day killed as much fowl as, with a little help beside, served the company almost a week. At which time, amongst other recreations, . . . many of the Indians [came] amongst us, [including] their greatest king Massasoit, with some ninety men, whom for three days we entertained and feasted. And they went out and killed five deer, which they brought to the plantation and bestowed on our governor, and upon the captain and others.
>
> And although it be not always so plentiful as it was at this time with us, yet by the goodness of God, we are so far from want that we often wish you partakers of our plenty.[1]

Lament and Prayer

However, it is also important to admit that not everyone recalls that first Plymouth Colony harvest feast with the same gratitude. In fact, the colonists' first taste of "Indian corn" came earlier out of a buried cache they plundered from a local burial site. With such disrespectful behavior, it was not long before the relationship between the Native Americans—who had lived there for thousands of years—and the newly arrived Europeans deteriorated as the interlopers claimed more and more land until war broke out in 1657, killing 5,000 people, three quarters of whom were Native Americans.

Swindled agreements, unfulfilled promises, outright theft of land and resources, and broken treaties have far too often characterized the way Native Americans have been treated ever since.

And yet, all of us who are not Native American Indians still benefit from these acquisitions in one way or another. For that reason, it is right and good for us to confess the condition we find ourselves in, asking God for mercy, and praying like the Prophet Amos: "Let justice roll down like waters and righteousness like an ever-flowing stream" (Amos 5:24, NASB).

At some point during your Thanksgiving celebration reflect honestly with your family on both the positive as well as the sad aspects of our history. And then lead them in an appropriate prayer.

Other Countries' Days of Thanksgiving Celebrations

It's also worth noting that a "thanksgiving day" is not a uniquely American holiday. Here are some other countries that have also set aside days to give thanks.

---

1 From a letter written by colonist Edward Winslow, dated December 12, 1621, and published in *Mourt's Relations*, by George Morton, 1622, London.

Brazil, *Dia Nacional de Acao de Gracas*, fourth Thursday of November.

British Isles, Lammas Day, a harvest festival on August 1.

Canada, Thanksgiving Day or *Fete de Grace*, or Harvest Home Festival, second Monday in October.

Germany, *Erntedankfest*, first Sunday in October.

Israel, *Sukkot*, Feast of Booths, the fifth day after Yom Kippur.

Japan, Labor Thanksgiving Day, November 23.

Korea, *Chusok*, fifteenth day of the eighth lunar month of the traditional Korean calendar.

Liberia, Thanksgiving Day, first Thursday in November.

Mexico, Independence Day, September 16.

Switzerland, The Federal Day of Thanks, Penance, and Prayer, third Sunday in September.

Give Thanks!

However you celebrate this day, *don't forget to give thanks.* The fact that we do not deserve our blessings is reason to be all the more thankful and humble. After all, it's not "*what* we have" so much as "*how* we hold it" that give us reason to celebrate with thanksgiving while we share with others. Consider this proverb:

> Better a little with the fear of the LORD than great wealth with turmoil. Better a meal of vegetables where there is love than a fattened calf with hatred (Proverbs 15:16–17, NIV).

Discuss with your family members: "What do you think this proverb means for *our* family? Are we focusing too much on our problems and not enough on our blessings? Are there family quarrels that need to be mended so we can truly give thanks?"

Expand Your Table

The whole family is coming for Thanksgiving? Great! But consider adding a few international students from the local college, a few singles from church, or the older couple down the street whose children live in distant states.

At the first Thanksgiving in 1621, Native Americans and European immigrants sat down at the same table and broke bread together. Why not invite a family from a culture or ethnic group different from your own to share Thanksgiving Day with your family? Let each family bring traditional dishes from their own culture. Listen to one another's stories. It will be a Thanksgiving Day you will never forget.

The family can't come this year? Quit moping! Volunteer to serve Thanksgiving dinner at a local homeless shelter, soup kitchen, or other ministry that serves the elderly, the lonely, or the poor. Don't just dish out food. Sit and talk with the guests. Play checkers or cards. You will not only be a blessing, but you will be blessed!

A Thanksgiving Mural

Tack a long piece of newsprint or a large poster board somewhere near the Thanksgiving table with colorful markers nearby. Encourage family and guests to write their thanksgivings on the mural during the day—no limit! Little ones can draw pictures. Date the mural and save it until the following year . . . then bring it out for everyone to enjoy before starting a new one.

Popcorn Praise

Before serving the food at your Thanksgiving dinner, place three kernels of popcorn on each dinner plate, then pass around a bowl, inviting each person to tell three things he or she is thankful for as they place their kernels in the bowl. You might assist younger children by suggesting categories: family, God, something fun.

Or . . . pass the bowl at three different times during the meal—before it begins, during the meal, when time for dessert. Pick a theme for the thanksgivings each time: "Something that happened this past year" . . . "Why you are thankful for the person sitting next to you" . . . "Something you are looking forward to" . . . etc.

A Family Advent Celebration

Like Jodi Baxter, you may sometimes feel pushed into Christmas by the frenzy and commercialism of the season without a moment to consider the magnitude of God being born on earth to live among us. For centuries, many Christians have slowed their hectic lives during the four weeks before Christmas to focus on the reason for the season by celebrating Advent—a word that means "coming" or "arriving"—a time of reflecting on Israel's long wait for a Messiah in order to prepare ourselves to celebrate His coming. Because of its ancient origin, there are many variations in the tradition, but "Ready My Heart," a simple carol by Lois Shuford, captures the essence well.

Ready my heart for the birth of Emmanuel
Ready my soul for the Prince of Peace.
Heap the straw of my life for His body to lie on,
Light the candle of hope. Let the Child come in.
Alleluia, Alleluia,
Alleluia, Christ the Savior is born![2]

2 "Ready My Heart," © 1976, Lois Farley Shuford. All rights reserved. Used by permission. Available on CD by Steve Bell, *The Feast of Seasons*, © 1995 www.signpostmusic.com.

The Advent Wreath

In the center of your table, construct a wreath of evergreens or holly. (Artificial greens or a wreath of ceramic or wood is less flammable.) Evenly space four purple or red candles in holders around the perimeter. In the center of the wreath, place a large white candle that is 1-1/2” to 3” in diameter.

Traditionally, *purple* has been a color that reminds us of sorrow and repentance, but it is also the color of royalty. The *evergreens* remind us of the eternal life Jesus Christ brings as His gift to us. The glow from all the *candles* reminds us that Jesus is the light of the world.

- The first candle is often called the *Prophets' Candle* and is meant to signify the hope of Messiah.
- The second is the *Bethlehem Candle*, reminding us that God came in a humble manner.
- The third candle (sometimes pink to express joy) is the *Shepherds' Candle*.
- The fourth candle is the *Angels' Candle*, symbolizing the good news of peace they brought.
- The white candle is the *Christ Candle* to be lit on Christmas Eve or Christmas Day.

The Christmas Holiday Season

If you're like Jodi Baxter, the main character in the Yada Yada novels (it's a little scary how many "Jodies" are out there!), it probably feels as if you've barely recovered from the last holiday season—paid the bills, put away the decorations, discovered the forgotten wrapping paper still under the bed—when the holidays loom large on the calendar again. In fact, most stores don't even wait for Thanksgiving to start piping in nonstop Christmas carols, Santa Claus, and aisles full of . . . stuff.

Hopefully, it won't take a sprained ankle to slow you down long enough to think about how you want to celebrate the holidays this year.

Of course, if you want fancy decorating tips, last-minute gift ideas, or tantalizing menus for a seven-course meal, feel free to pick up one of the slick women's magazines at the grocery store checkout, take a few guilt trips that you're not doing enough . . . then go back to "doing the holidays" the same old way.

But if you'd like a few tips on celebrating the holiday season "the Yada Yada way," sit tight and take a bite!

Celebrating Advent

- Advent begins four Sundays before Christmas (usually the first Sunday after Thanksgiving).
- *On the first Sunday*, do the full celebration (see "A Family Advent Celebration" below) for that week together as a family. Repeat the Call and Response, read

the first week's scripture, light the first candle while saying its meaning and allowing it to burn during your meal, and sing the first verse of "O Come, O Come, Emmanuel." During the week, do an abbreviated version: Light the first candle each night while repeating its meaning and sing the first verse of "O Come, O Come, Emmanuel."

- On the *second, third, and fourth Sundays of Advent*, do that week's full celebration, adding the second, third, and fourth candle lightings as appropriate. On the weekdays of those weeks, do the shortened version of lighting all candles to date while saying their meanings but sing only that week's verse of "O Come, O Come, Emmanuel."
- Each Scripture passage is read only on its respective Sunday. The lighting of the candles, however, is added accumulatively until all the candles are burning together the fourth week and on Christmas.

First Week

Call and Response

LEADER: The people who walked in darkness have seen a great light.

ALL: Those who dwelled in a land of deep darkness, on them has light shined.

LEADER: For unto us a child is born, unto us a son is given, and the government shall be upon his shoulders.

ALL: And his name shall be called Wonderful Counselor, Mighty God, Everlasting Father, Prince of Peace.

Read the first Scripture: Isaiah 40:1–5.

Light the first candle and say:

I light this candle in memory of God's promise to send a Savior who will forgive our sins and bring peace and justice to a broken world.

Sing the first verse and refrain of "O Come, O Come, Emmanuel."

Second Week

Call and Response—repeat from the first week.

Light the first candle, repeat its meaning, and sing the first verse and refrain of "O Come, O Come, Emmanuel."

Read the second Scripture: John 8:12.

Light the second candle, and say:

I light this candle in memory of Jesus Christ, who is the light of the world.

Sing the second verse and refrain of "O Come, O Come, Emmanuel."

Third Week

Call and Response—repeat from the first week.

Light the first and second candles, repeat their meanings, and sing the respective verses of "O Come, O Come, Emmanuel."

Read the third Scripture: Luke 1:32–33.
Light the third candle, and say:
I light this candle in memory of Jesus, born of the house of David, in the town of Bethlehem.
Sing the third verse and refrain of "O Come, O Come, Emmanuel."

Fourth Week

Call and Response—repeat from the first week.
Light the first three candles, repeat their meanings, and sing the respective verses of "O Come, O Come, Emmanuel."

Read the fourth Scripture: Revelation 5:9–10
Light the fourth candle, and say:
I light this candle for Jesus Christ who was born to be Lord of the nations.
Sing the fourth verse and refrain of "O Come, O Come, Emmanuel."

Christmas Day

Call and Response—repeat from the first week.
Light the first four candles, repeating their meanings, and sing the respective verses of "O Come, O Come, Emmanuel."

O Come, O Come, Emmanuel

1. O come, O come, Emmanuel,
And ransom captive Israel,
That mourns in lonely exile here,
Until the Son of God appears.

Refrain:
Rejoice! Rejoice! Emmanuel
Shall come to thee, O Israel.

2. O come, Thou Dayspring, come and cheer
Our spirits by Thine advent here;
Disperse the gloomy clouds of night
And death's dark shadows put to flight.

3. O come, Thou Key of David, come
And open wide our heavenly home.
Make safe the way that leads on high,
And close the path to misery.

4. O come, Desire of nations, bind
All peoples in one heart and mind.
Bid envy, strife, and quarrels cease.
Fill the whole world with heaven's peace.[1]

1 Latin hymn from the twelfth century, translated by John M. Neale, 1851. The original hymn had seven or eight verses. These four match the weekly themes best.

Read the Christmas Scripture: Luke 2:1–20.

Light the Christmas candle. Say:

I light this candle for Jesus Christ, who was born in a manger on Christmas Day.

Sing "Away in a Manger."

Suggestions:

- Doing the celebration each day will undoubtedly use up your candles, but the daily meditation can be meaningful, so just replace them with new ones.
- Let each child and/or parent be responsible for lighting one particular candle and saying what it means (e.g., oldest child lights first candle, second child second candle, a parent lights third candle, etc.).
- If the full Advent celebration is too long for your family, just read the new scripture and light the new candle each week.

Hanukkah
The Festival of Lights

Sometime in the month of December. (An eight-day festival that begins on the twenty-fifth day in the month of Kislev on the Jewish calendar.) The actual date for any particular year can be found online by searching: "When does Hanukkah begin this year?"

Background

Hanukkah commemorates the restoration of temple worship by Judas Maccabee and his followers after Jerusalem had been captured and the temple desecrated by Syrian invaders (an event which happened between the Old and New Testaments, and is recounted in the Talmud, as well as by Josephus the historian). According to tradition, as the temple was being cleaned out, only a small amount of oil was found to light the temple lamps, enough for one day. But miraculously, the lamps stayed lit for eight days until more oil could be found. Ever since, this holiday is celebrated with the lighting of the *menorah*, a lampstand with nine candles—eight to represent each day of the miracle and a central one to light the others.

Meaning for Christians

Jesus called Himself the Light of the World

(see John 8:12; John 9:3-5), and He encourages His followers to be lights in this world (Matthew 5:14-16).

Ways to Celebrate

If possible, purchase a menorah lamp stand and the appropriate candles to fit into it. Or create your own "menorah" with eight candles, plus one (the shamash) to light the others. On the first evening of Hannukah, light the candle on the far right of the menorah. On each successive evening, light an additional candle until all eight candles are burning.

Talk with your children about miracles—the miracles in the Bible, and the miracles we experience in our own lives. Say this blessing as you light that evening's candle: "Blessed are you, Lord our God, King of the universe, who performed miracles for our ancestors, at this season, in days past." And add: "And who continues to bless us with the miracles of life, of love, of health, of family."

Playing with a Dreidel—a spinning top—is a traditional game at Hannukah. On the Dreidel are four Hebrew letters: *Nun, Gimel, Hei,* and *Shin.* (The letters stand for *"Nes Gadol Hayah Sham,"* or *"A great miracle happened here."*)

How to play: Each player puts the same amount of a treat—e.g., nuts, raisins, chocolate kisses, or peppermints, etc.—into the middle. This is called "The Pot." Each player takes a turn spinning the Dreidel. Whichever letter the Dreidel lands on decides what you have to do. Whoever has the most treats in the end wins the game—though sharing them would be completely within the spirit of the season!

Nun (נ): You get none of The Pot.

Gimel (ג): You get ALL of The Pot.

Hei (ה): You get half of The Pot.

Shin (ש): You must add one more treat to The Pot.

Section 2
Anytime Celebrations . . .

What was it Charles Dickens said? *"It was the best of times. It was the worst of times."* All of us could probably say the same thing—about being a teenager *(the bloom of youth! the bloom of zits!)* . . . falling in love *(falling in, falling out)* . . . raising kids *(we love 'em! we hate 'em!)* . . . going on vacation *(ack! don't even get me started).*

Or pick a decade, any decade. The Fifties? *A nostalgic decade for many Americans—unless you were black and still battling Jim Crow laws.* The Sixties? *Hoo boy! Hula hoops and rock 'n roll!—and angry war protesters and civil rights marches.*

The reality is: God never promised any of us a rose garden. Wait. Take that back. God *did* promise us a rose garden. Joy and beauty! Love and laughter. But as a reminder that we live in a fallen world, even roses have thorns. Many times in our lives, joy and sorrow seem to walk hand in hand.

The good news is, even in the darkest times, there are rays of hope and beauty. Reason enough to celebrate—just like the Yada Yada sisters did, even though they sure enough did get caught up in some messes!

Celebrating Milestones

In the first *Yada Yada Prayer Group* novel, the sisters celebrated a major milestone for Florida: "Five years saved and five years sober!" Well, why not? At birthdays and anniversaries, we celebrate those milestones in a person's life, to honor that person or a marriage, to reflect on God's goodness in the past and look forward to the future.

Why not other milestones? Little people and big people need encouragement, and celebrations are a great way to encourage someone. Like Sophea . . .

Sophea's Story

Several years ago, our family was privileged to include a Cambodian foster daughter. Sophea had been born in a refugee camp. When her family finally arrived in the U.S., Sophea was nine years old but had never attended school. Tiny and petite, she looked six, so she fit right into the first grade. No problem . . . until several years later when her middle school teachers found out she was fifteen, going into seventh grade. *No way!* they said—and bumped her up into high school. Of course, she wasn't prepared, had no idea what was going on in her classes, so she started skipping school and hanging out on the street. Her mother, who spoke little English and didn't understand how to navigate American culture, was tearing her hair out and ready to marry her off.

Long story short, Sophea came to live with us in the middle of her freshman year. Her schooling was a mess, but we started with the first requirement for living with us:

Go to school every day.

No skipping.

It was a struggle. Temptation to skip was great. But Sophea wanted to live with us, so she was in school every day. Her grades were terrible. But on the last day of that school semester, she had *perfect attendance*. So . . .

We celebrated! We took her out to dinner. We gave her flowers. We told her we were proud of her. We bragged on her to our church. And when she walked across the platform three years later to get her high school diploma, we were there cheering for her.

So, Celebrate Those Milestones!

It may seem a little silly to have "graduations" from kindergarten, but even small events and milestones may be worth celebrating—especially if a celebration honors someone who might otherwise be overlooked. Some events worth celebrating:

- A surprise Appreciation Party for the janitor at your child's school
- Balloons and snacks for the garbage truck guys—anytime, or near Labor Day
- A Thank You Celebration for the nurses who took care of you in your last hospitalization
- A "You Did It!" party for someone who quit smoking
- The One-Year Anniversary of anything!—keeping a job, your new prayer group, beating cancer, losing excess weight and keeping it off . . . whatever!
- Completing a marathon (even if your runner didn't "win")
- A backyard barbecue for the New Neighbor
- A school drop-out who finally gets his or her G.E.D.

. . . Or, as Yo-Yo might say, "Who needs an excuse to party?"

Make the Celebration Appropriate to the Occasion

Don't give your kids a blow-out party for every minor achievement. A simple, "I'm proud of you," might be all that's needed. But don't take everything for granted, either. Pulling that D up to an A-minus is a big deal and took hard work. So, celebrate!

Flowers, an inexpensive gift, a card, a

coupon for a movie, or a special dessert are wonderful ways to say, "Thank you!"

Food . . . Did we mention food? Take a milestone in someone's life, invite friends, *add food*, and *voila!* Instant party!

Naming and Blessing

Ever since Jodi Baxter discovered the meaning of her name ("God is gracious") at a time when she needed a touch of God's grace (see "*The Yada Yada Prayer Group Gets Down*," Book 2, chapter 15), she's been digging up the meanings for people's names and finding ways to *bless* that person, just as she did for Mark Smith at the hospital in *The Yada Yada Prayer Group Gets Tough* (Book 4). To tell you the truth, she's on to something.

"Naming" and "blessing" are two important concepts in Scripture. For one thing, God has many names, each one revealing an important aspect of His character (see page 51). For another thing, our names are important to God! At times, God gave a new name to a man or woman when their spiritual life direction changed—e.g., *Abram* ("exalted father") to *Abraham* ("father of many nations"); Sarai (quarrelsome) to Sarah (princess); Jesus changed Simon's name ("he who hears") to Peter, which means "rock"; Saul (a Hebrew name) became Paul (a Roman name) as the apostle took the Gospel to the Gentiles.

Why are names so important? To know and use a person's name, that which identifies each of us as a unique individual, is to take the first step toward a personal relationship. And the opposite is true. One way to hold a person at arm's length is to think of them as "that girl" or "those kids" rather than bother to know them by name.

The amazing thing is that *God knows each one of us by name.* And He longs to bless us! Not just generically, but specifically, by name! You. Me.

Biblical Background

Use the following Scriptures (1) as a foundation for some of the celebrations and activities below, (2) for a Bible study with *your* "Yada Yada Prayer Group," or (3) simply as fodder for your own reflection.

- ***God knows us by name!*** See Isaiah 49:1 (He knew our name before we were born!) and Isaiah 49:14-16. In v. 16, the New Living Translation uses the phrase, "written *your name* on the palms of my hand," which is also implied in all the other translations when it says, "*engraved you* on the palms of my hands" (NIV), "*inscribed you* on the palms of My hands" (NKJV), and "*graven thee* on the palms of my hands" (KJV). Think about it. If our *names* are *engraved* on the hands of God, Christ took our names with Him to the cross when He willingly spread out His hands . . . and died for our sins.

- ***God calls us by name!*** See Isaiah 43:1. His redemption is not generic for "the whole world," but for us individually *by name.*
- ***Isaac blessed his two sons.*** See Genesis 27:1-40. Isaac blessed even the youngest who fooled his father into thinking he was the eldest; and even the eldest who so carelessly gave away his birthright.
- ***Jacob wrestled with an angel (or God Himself) until he got a blessing (and a new name!).*** See Genesis 32:22-32. For the rest of his life he had a limp to prove it!
- ***Moses blessed each of the tribes of Israel by name.*** See Deuteronomy 33. Note the *specific* prophetic blessing for each tribe!
- ***John the Baptist was prophetically named before his birth, and prophetically blessed at his naming ceremony.*** See Luke 1:5-25; 57-80.
- ***Jesus was prophetically named before He was born.*** See Luke 1:26-38.
- ***The infant Jesus was prophetically blessed by Simeon and Anna in the temple.*** See Luke 2:21-40.
- ***Jesus laid hands on and blessed the children.*** See Mark 10:13-16. It's easy to imagine Jesus not only touching each head tenderly, but calling the children by name as each child was blessed.

A Blessing Shower

So why not give a Blessing Shower for the next baby-to-be-born among your family or friends, instead of the usual baby-gifts-and-shower-games party? Nothing wrong with the latter, but a Blessing Shower can be very meaningful.

With ultrasound and sonograms so common, many couples know the sex of their baby before it's born and have already picked out The Name. (If not, why not throw the Blessing Shower *after* the baby is born when sex and name are known—and then the guest of honor can be present!)

- When you invite the shower guests, provide an 8½ x 11-inch sheet of paper (there are many pretty papers available at stores that sell office or paper supplies!) and ask them to write or print out a *blessing* for the child. (*Option*: Or this could be done when guests arrive, providing pretty paper and fine-tipped colored markers to write a blessing as an activity.)
- At the shower, have each guest read their blessing one by one and present it to the parent. One of the blessings might include the *meanings* of the child's first and middle names (see page 50).
- Collect all the blessings into a presentation folder or notebook to give to the parents after the shower. Slipping the pages into three-hole clear plastic sheet protectors is an easy way to protect the pages and make a notebook.
- *Optional:* Include blessings for the parents!
- Oh, go ahead and let guests bring baby gifts, too—but keep the emphasis on *blessing* the new child, a gift that will be remembered long after the rattles are lost and the cute outfits outgrown.

Make Name-Meaning Bookmarks

Readers of the Yada Yada novels have written to say that Jodi's "name meanings" have inspired them to make bookmarks as gifts for the sisters in their prayer groups, with the name of each sister on a bookmark, along with the meaning of her name. What a wonderful idea! (Thank you, readers, who have shared this idea!) Here are a few ideas for making bookmarks:

Laminated Paper Bookmarks

- Using "fun fonts" on your computer, write out each person's name with the name meaning underneath, centering the type and using different colors for the name and its meaning.
- The size of the fonts should be approximately 36-point type for the name, and 26 point type for the meaning of the name (depending on the font).
- Leave adequate space between names so that when cut apart horizontally (and then turned lengthwise), this part of each bookmark is approximately 1¾ inches wide. Print on scrap paper until you get what you want. Then . . .
- Print out names on a color printer, using heavy white paper or card stock, if possible.
- Cut this part of the bookmark so it measures approximately 6¼ inches long and 1¾ inches wide.
- Now cut a piece of heavy colored paper 6½ inches long and 2¼ inches wide. Glue the "name" piece to the larger colored piece.
- For the back side, once again using "fun fonts" and colors, type out a portion of Isaiah 43:1: "I have called *you* by your

name, you *are* Mine" (NKJV). Font size should be around 16-20-point type. Print out on heavy white paper or card stock using a color printer. Cut out Scripture using the same dimensions as the front side of the bookmark (e.g., 6¼ inches long and 1¾ inches wide). Glue to the backside of the bookmark.

- Add cute stickers (hearts, swirls, flowers, stars, whatever) if you wish.
- Laminate the whole bookmark, front and back. Punch a hole near the top and thread a thin ribbon through it, tying a knot so the ribbon ends hang 3 to 4 inches long.

Embroidered Bookmark

- If you like to embroider or cross stitch, cut a piece of sturdy (but not too heavy) material approximately 7 inches long and 5 inches wide. (This allows the bookmark material to be folded once lengthwise and the edges turned under ¼ inch and hemmed). You might want to iron the fold and the to-be-hemmed edges before you embroider so you know where to center your design on one side.
- Using a light pencil, draw the name you wish to embroider, and the meaning underneath.
- Embroider or cross-stitch along the pencil markings, using a complimentary color for the embroidery thread. Add any designs you'd like.
- Now fold the length of material in half (to hide the back of the embroidery—usually a mess!). Hand stitch or machine stitch the top, long side edge, and bottom together (turned under at least ¼ inch). A zig-zag machine stitch can make a pretty edge all the way around.
- Leave as is, or add a ribbon or thin cord at one end before stitching the sides together.

Other Ways to Use Names and Their Meanings

Family Reunions

As a way to bless the members of your family, look up the meanings of their names (see page 50). Create a "page" for each family member on your computer with his or her name and its meaning, using "fun fonts" on your computer (or fonts that capture a person's personality). Print each person's "name page" on paper with a pretty border (can be purchased in packs at any office or stationery store), roll them up like a scroll, tie with ribbon, and present their name and its meaning at one of your family gatherings.

Use the meaning of each person's name to bless or encourage him or her as you give the scrolls, e.g: "David, your name means 'beloved'—and you are definitely 'beloved' by me and the rest of this family" . . . "Connie, your name means 'constancy, firmness.' We already know that when this little girl makes up her mind, it's set in cement! Might drive us crazy, but it can be a good thing" . . . etc.

Birthday or Encouragement Cards

If you're good at making handmade or computer-generated cards, consider using the person's name and its meaning as a way to bless and encourage the recipient. E.g.: "Maggie ~ 'Pearl' . . . "Maggie, even when the grit of life gets into the gears, you always seem to be able to turn little problems into pearls of wisdom and beauty."

A Quilt Square for a Friendship, Wedding, or Baby Quilt

See instructions for making a Friendship Quilt, page 55. Embroider the middle quilt square with the names of the wedding couple or the name of the newborn and the meanings of the name(s) as well.

Child's Pillow

A "Name Pillow" makes a great baby gift for a newborn, or even as a birthday gift for an older child. Such a pillow often becomes a favorite "friend" to a child, good for trips or overnights away from home.

Sew a simple pillowcase to cover a child-size pillow (or make a small pillow with a finished size approximately 12 x 9 inches that can be stuffed with foam or other hypoallergenic "stuffing material" and sewn closed on all sides). But before sewing or stuffing, embroider the child's name, birth date, and meaning of the child's name on the pillowcase. Possibilities are endless for colorful material, lacey edgings, and size of the pillow.

Resources for Names

There are baby name books galore to help parents pick out a name for their new baby. But there are helpful web sites, too—especially when you already know the name and want to find out its meaning. The Internet is especially helpful when searching for names from various cultures that might not be included in a specific book.

- **Baby Name Network** (www.babynamenetwork.com) not only tells you the most popular names in the U.S. by decade, but also has links to names from countries all over the world.
- **Behind the Name** (www.behindthename.com) provides "an etymology and history of first names," and is another excellent site to explore names from all over the world.
- **Andy the Name Bender** (www.wirewriter.com) not only can help you find a name and its meaning, but he makes personalized "name" jewelry, too!
- **Resources for Life** (www.resourcesforlife.com/docs/item2002) provides a Directory of Hebrew and Bible Name Meanings.

Exploring the Names of God

In the Old Testament, and often in the New, the meaning of a name had everything to do with why a child was given a certain name. The name sometimes reflected the life circumstances of the parent (e.g., the name Jabez means "pain"—see 1 Chronicles 4:9), a physical feature or character trait (e.g., Esau means "red" or "ruddy"; Jacob means "grabber"—see Genesis 25:19-26), or a promise from God (e.g., the name Ishmael means "God hears"—see Genesis 16:11).

But as you read the Scriptures, you will realize that our God has many names, each one revealing a new aspect of God's character. If you have never before explored the names of God and their meanings, run—don't walk—to your favorite bookstore or get online and order the following:

- ***Praying the Names of God*** by Ann Spangler (Zondervan Publishers, Grand Rapids, MI) © 2004. This book is a daily guide to exploring and praying *according to the meaning* of God's names. Great for personal or group study.
- ***The Glorious Names of God*** by Mary Foxwell Loeks (Baker Books, Grand Rapids, MI) © 1986. This book is *out of print,* but there are "used" (still often new) copies for sale on www.amazon.com. Includes many more names than the more recent book above.

"Coming of Age" Celebrations

"Coming of age" rituals and ceremonies mark the transition from childhood to adulthood in cultures all over the world. Many are religious in nature and mark spiritual awareness and maturity; others coincide with reaching sexual maturity; still others simply acknowledge reaching the legal age of adulthood. A few examples:

For Catholics and Episcopal/Anglican churches, the Sacrament of Confirmation at age 13 is preceded by instruction in the *catechisms* of the church and confers "sanctifying grace" on youth entering their adolescence. For other Protestant denominations who practice infant baptism, it may be called a Rite of Confirmation, a symbol of a maturing faith.

Other Christian congregations wait for the "age of accountability" (around age 12) to be eligible to receive baptism and partake of "communion" or The Lord's Supper based on a personal confession of faith. Some churches use this time to present a Bible to the twelve-year-old during a worship service, acknowledging they are entering the time when they will be exploring the Scriptures on their own and making more mature decisions regarding their faith. (Some families choose to make it a larger celebration, similar to the Jewish *Bar* or *Bat Mitzvah* below.)

For Jewish youth, the "age of maturity" is celebrated with a *Bar Mitzvah* (for boys

age 13) and a *Bat Mitzvah* (for girls age 12). The term "Mitzvah" means "one to whom the commandments apply." The religious service, in which the young man (or woman) reads from the Torah and leads part of the service, is attended by family, friends, and the larger community, and is usually followed by a lavish party. (Recently, some Jewish youth are choosing to raise money for charitable causes at their Bar or Bat Mitzvahs, rather than the usual extravagant gifts—a hopeful trend among the young.)

Tribal societies have long practiced a wide variety of "coming of age" rituals and rites of passage. These might include "walkabouts" (e.g., Australian aborigines) or other tests of skill and courage alone in the wilderness; scarification or tattoos or other bodily (and often painful) symbols of adulthood; being allowed to go with the men on a hunt and killing their first wild animal (to prove a boy is man enough to be a provider), etc.

The affluent classes in England, the U.S., and other European countries, still hold debutante balls when young women reach the age of 18. The original purpose of "debutante" (which means making one's "debut" or "coming out") was to present young women who had reached marriageable age to the families and eligible bachelors within a proscribed social circle or class. Today the purpose is somewhat broader, to present the young lady to the society in which she will hopefully remain active, as well as celebrate her accomplishments thus far and support her goals and dreams.

The legal age varies from country to country. In the United States, the legal age for voting, joining the armed forces, and getting married without parental consent is 18 (though the legal age for drinking alcohol is still 21). But the legal age at which one can get a driver's license is often 16—and is also the most common "age of consent" for consensual sexual intercourse. (Go figure!)

Other: Many young people in the United States do not have official coming of age celebrations, other than graduations from high school or college. Some consider experiences like Outward Bound (or other adventure-based programs for teens) as a kind of "rite of passage," especially for boys, as well as Sweet Sixteen birthday parties for girls—though neither of these involves official incorporation into "adult life" by the faith community or larger society.

If you're like Jodi Baxter (that's okay, you don't have to confess), you might have been oblivious to a major "coming of age" event celebrated not only in many Latin American countries, but in Latino communities throughout the United States—the *quinceañera*. But as the Baxters discovered, it can provide some meaningful ideas for celebrating that young woman growing up in your home . . .

The Quinceañera

The *quinceañera* (or *quinceañero* in Puerto Rico and Peru) stands for *quince años* or "fifteen years." Originally it was a time to acknowledge that a young woman was ready to leave home and be eligible for marriage. (In fact, the lavishness of the occasion sometimes resembles a wedding, but without the groom!) The tradition continues today, although with the more general purpose of marking the transition from childhood to womanhood.

Unlike the *debutante ball*, a *quinceañera* focuses on the individual "birthday girl." This is her Special Day, and she is The *Quinceañera*. Some of the meaningful traditions:

The Lady and Her Court

The *Quinceañera* wears a formal gown. The traditional color is pink, but today the color is simply "lady's choice."

She might choose 7 girls (friends, sisters, cousins) to be her *damas* ("ladies"), and 7 boys to be her *chambelánes* ("escorts"), wearing formal gowns and tuxedos. These 14 plus herself would equal 15—the magic number for the celebration. A more lavish *quinceañera* might include 14 girls and 14 boys, plus one more as her personal escort (can be a friend, cousin, or brother), i.e. fifteen couples—but many *quinceañeras* work perfectly well with fewer attendants.

Godparents are often chosen for the occasion.

Highlights of the Day

The celebration begins with a church ceremony (a mass, if the family is Catholic), which might include: a processional of the court, parents, godparents, and the *quinceañera* and her escort (if she has one); Scriptures focusing on character qualities and the responsibilities of adulthood; prayers of blessing by the godparents, priest, or minister; favorite hymns or songs chosen by the *Quinceañera*; and the presentation of special gifts and what they mean.

Next comes a reception, kicking off the festivities with food, music, and dance! This might involve an elaborate sit-down dinner, or simply a buffet table with plenty of food and drink.

The first dance is for the *Quinceañera* and her father alone, traditionally a waltz. (In the absence of father, an honored male relative fulfills this role.) Traditional *quinceañera* songs, such as *De Niña a Mujer* ("From Childhood to Womanhood") or *Le Ultima Muñeca* ("The Last Doll") highlight this very special father/daughter waltz.

The *Quinceañera* might be wearing flats during the church ceremony, but after the dance with her father, she ceremoniously changes from flats to heels, signifying her becoming a young woman.

The *Quinceañera* and her court then perform a specially choreographed dance they have been practicing—from a traditional waltz to a simple line dance or a more modern dance routine—a surprise for the invited guests.

The *Quinceañera Doll* is used as a decoration (often dressed in a similar gown to the guest of honor) and a keepsake, symbolizing the young lady's last doll. She might also throw an inexpensive Barbie-type doll (or any other) to the younger set (much as a bride throws her garter), symbolizing leaving her childhood behind.

Special Gifts and their Meanings

Tiara. The *quinceañera* wears a tiara because she is a "princess" in God's eyes, His beloved daughter. This may actually be part of the ceremony, with her parents or godparents "crowning" the young lady.

Ring. May symbolize a vow to remain a virgin until marriage. Also represents the unending cycle of life, the emergence of the young woman's abilities, and her future contributions to society.

Earrings. A reminder to *listen* to the voice of God through His Word, and to listen responsively to others around her.

Cross necklace. Symbolizes her faith in God.

Bible, Prayer Book, or Book of Devotions. Not just a reminder, but resources to help her build her faith on the Word of God and prayer.

Traditional Food

What's traditional? That depends on the country! But if you are trying to recreate a Mexican *quinceañera*, you can't go wrong with a Mexican buffet. Guests can choose what they want to eat and there's not as much waste. Of course, there is *birria* (Mexican stew) and *chicken mole*, both served over rice. (Or *mole poblano* served over chicken or turkey.) But there are also simpler foods, such as *taquitos*—beef or chicken mixture rolled up in a corn tortilla, fried lightly, and served with salsa, sour cream, or guacamole. (Check online for recipes!)

Make It Your Own

The whole point of a *quinceañera* is to celebrate the young girl moving into womanhood. Use these ideas to create your own celebration, use what's meaningful to you and your family, and add to them. That's what learning from other cultures and sharing traditions is all about—enriching our lives and enlarging our family of faith.

A Friendship or Wedding Quilt

A Friendship Quilt can be a wonderful way to celebrate a wedding or anniversary—or any other special occasion where a group of friends and family want to remind a sister, friend, or couple just how many people love them.

The Basic Idea

Muslin squares of material are given to friends and family to decorate in a design of their choosing with embroidery, cross-stitch, or appliqué. Then the squares are collected, sewn together in strips with narrow sashes of colorful material separating each square, then the strips are sewn together to make a large block of squares which represents the body of the quilt. A border of material is added around the block of squares, then batting (the filling) and material for the back side are added, held together with binding around the outer edge. (See pattern on page 57.)

When the front and back of the quilt have been sewn together, it can then either be "tied" with yarn at the corners of all the squares, "quilted" by simple line stitching in the sashes and borders with thread that *matches* the color of the material so it is basically invisible, or actually quilted with little designs by an experienced quilter, again using *matching* thread so as not to compete with the embroidered designs.

Overwhelmed? Don't be! Take the plunge! It'll be a gift never to be forgotten—either by the givers or the receiver.

Material Needed

Color scheme: Decide what your color scheme is going to be. Consider your friend's tastes—or take her along to help choose the material if it's not a surprise. Generally, the *sashes* between the squares and the *first border* should be a solid color, while the *outside border* can be a complimentary pattern. The *back of the quilt* can either be plain or patterned, but the *binding edge* should be a solid color (e.g., the same as the sashes or picking up a contrasting color from the pattern). Or . . . mix and match your own ideas!

Size of the quilt: These instructions are for a *queen-size quilt with 42 squares*—six across and seven down—which can be used as a bed coverlet or (as often happens) a large wall hanging. Obviously, you can make a Friendship Quilt of any size, or even a much-smaller wall hanging. (You will need a sewing friend who can estimate the amount of material needed!)

Material: Use good quality 100-percent cotton—and be sure to wash it before cutting! All amounts are based on 45-inch material, unless otherwise noted.

The muslin squares: You will need 3¼ yards of 45-inch muslin. After washing the material, cut muslin into forty-two 10½ inch squares. The finished size of the squares *after hemming* will be 9 inches (leaving room for a ¾ inch hem all the way around).

For sashes and first border: You will need 1⅛ yards of 45-inch material for the sashes and 1⅝ yards for the first border—a total of 2¾ yards (or 3 yards on the safe side!). Cut sashes and first border into 3½ inch strips, which allows for a ¾ inch hem on either side. The *finished* width will be 2½ inches.

Outside border: You will need 2½ yards of 45-inch material for the outside border. Cut border strips 6 inches wide, allowing for a ¾-inch hem on the inside edge only! (The outside edge will be "hemmed" by the binding edge.) The *finished* width of the outside border will be 5¼ inches.

Binding edge: You will need 1⅛ yards of 45-inch material for the binding edge, if you use a contrasting color.

Back of quilt: You will need 3 yards of 90-inch material; 6 yards of 45-inch material; or 9 yards of 33-inch material. The last two amounts, obviously, will need to be pieced to cover the back. The *finished size of the quilt* (and the *back*) will be 87-inches wide and 99-inches long.

Option: If you want to make a smaller quilt—say, 30 squares (5 across and 6 down)—the finished size will be 70½ inches across and 82-inches long. The sashes and borders can be adjusted proportionally. *Or* you could add another border to compensate for the fewer number of squares.

Time Frame

Allow two to three months for sending out the muslin squares to friends and family and getting them back (allowing six to eight weeks for individuals to decorate their square). If past experience counts for anything, you might want to add another four weeks to nag procrastinators!

Allow *at least* three months for piecing the quilt together and quilting it. (Ask whoever is doing the piecing/quilting how much time they will need.)

Total from start to finish: *Six months* is a good guesstimate!

Sending out the Squares

- Draw up your list of friends and family.
- Write a letter giving instructions to accompany each muslin quilt square:
- Attach small swatches of the border materials to the letter and ask them to choose complimentary colors for their design.
- They may use embroidery, cross-stitch, or appliqué. (Fabric crayons or paints should be avoided.) Photos can also be used—ask your favorite T-shirt place how to do it.
- Leave at least a 1½ inch border *around all sides* of their square.

- Please embroider their *name* somewhere on the design.
- Give them a *deadline* when to return the finished square to you.
- Ask them to let you know ASAP if they will not be able to do a square (and return the material) so that you can find a replacement. (Some families are glad to do two squares.)
- *Optional:* Ask friends and family to contribute $5 to $10 per square to help with the cost of the material and quilting.

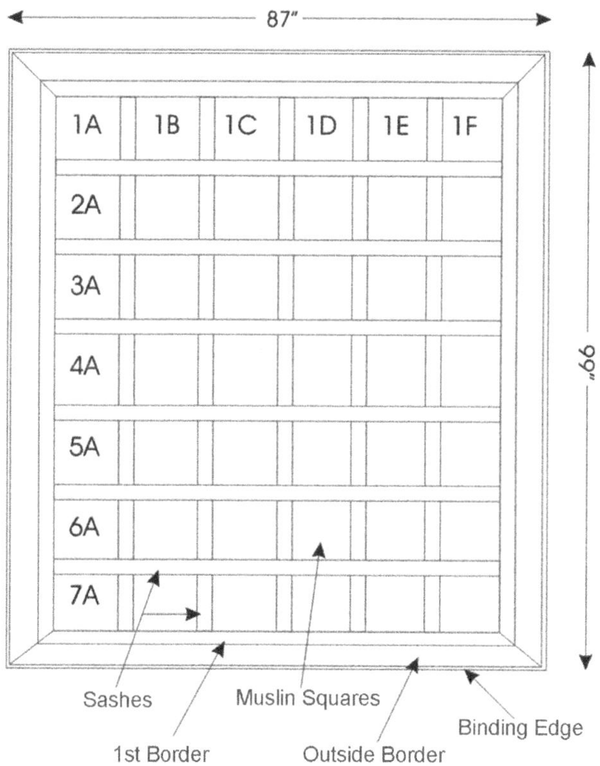

Putting the Quilt Together

As the squares are returned, place each one in a gallon-size zip-lock baggie. This protects the squares and allows you to label each one where it should be positioned in the quilt.

Once you have received all the decorated squares (*ahem* . . . patience, patience!), lay them out on the floor in rows (e.g., six across and seven down). Try to balance the designs in a pleasing overall pattern.

Then label the baggies so the person who sews it together (the quilter) will know where to place each square, using 1, 2, 3, etc. for the horizontal rows, and A, B, C, etc. for the vertical rows. (I.e., the top horizontal row would be labeled: 1A, 1B, 1C, 1D, 1E, 1F. The next row would be 2A, 2B, 2C, etc. See accompanying diagram.)

Reverently deliver the squares-in-baggies and all the other material to the person who is going to put the quilt together, along with the pattern and instructions for cutting the sashes, borders, back, and binding (see "Material Needed" on pages 55-56). This might be the same person who will do the quilting . . . or not.

If the quilt is going to be hung for display purposes at the wedding (or even on the wall at home), ask for a "rod pocket" to be attached to the back along the top edge of the quilt, using the same color material as the backing. This is simply a long strip of material, approximately 6 inches wide, machine-hemmed along both sides, and then hand-stitched to the back of the quilt to allow for a sturdy rod (wood or metal) to be slipped through.

When the entire quilt has been put together, then it's time for the "quilting." (See quilting ideas under "The Basic Idea," page 55.) This can be done as a "gift" by a relative or friend who has quilting skills, or you may need to hire an experienced quilter.

Displaying the Quilt

Hanging the quilt at the wedding reception or anniversary party is a wonderful way to share this wonderful gift of friendship. (See "rod pocket," bottom of page 57.)

Make a "Map to the Quilt" to display: Either by hand or on your computer, create a "grid" with the exact number of quilt squares (e.g. six across and seven down; or five across and six down; etc.). Fill in each square with a brief description of the quilt square on one line, and the name of the person who made it right below (e.g. "Basket of flowers, Jane Doe"). Print out the "map" on pretty paper and frame one for the guest(s) of honor. Make copies for anyone who would like one—especially those who contributed to the quilt!

Wahoo! You did it! Now it's *really* time to celebrate!

A House Blessing

In *The Yada Yada Prayer Group Gets Caught* (Book 5), both Chanda and Florida celebrate new homes. Chanda bought a home in an upscale neighborhood; the Hickman's are renting a "fixer upper." But both homes are gifts from God, and the Yada Yada sisters wanted to celebrate His goodness by having a "House Blessing."

That's right. A *House Blessing* is different than a "house warming," where the primary idea is to throw a party, invite all your friends to see your new digs, hoping they'll all bring gifts (new towels, candles, a bottle of wine) or, better yet, all chip in on a new gas grill.

But a House Blessing calls together family and friends not only to thank God for His provision of a roof over our heads, but to *dedicate* this home to the glory of God. A House Blessing acknowledges that even our everyday life is sacramental, and our homes are a holy space. Family and friends gather to seek God's protection on this home and its inhabitants, and to ask God's blessing, not just on the physical space, but on all that is said and done within its walls.

When Should You Have a House Blessing?

Moving into a new home, apartment, or condo is certainly a good time to celebrate with a House Blessing. But *any* home, even one you've lived in for years, is a candidate.

But here's the thing: don't invite folks to come "bless your mess." Preparing for a House Blessing can be an important time to get your rooms in order, and to rethink the way your family relates to one another at home. What do people see and hear when they walk into your home—people screaming at each other? dirty dishes everywhere? the TV droning twelve hours a day?

No, no, no, I'm not saying you have to create a photo op for *House Beautiful*. Kids *will* be kids (translation: noisy and messy), and we all prefer a "lived in" look rather than a museum piece. But something important happens when we invite Jesus to be Lord of our homes and family life, when we dedicate the place we live and the *way* we live every day to His glory.

So, let's begin. The ideas below can be used by themselves or in combination for *your* house blessing!

Bless This House

How you conduct your House Blessing depends somewhat on the number of people involved, as well as your own church traditions.

If you have invited your pastor, you might want to ask him or her to begin the prayers before moving throughout the house, and again to offer the closing prayer. But give opportunity for your friends and family members to also read Scriptures and/or offer prayers of blessing throughout the house as well.

If your group is not large (5-10 people), the whole group can move together from room to room throughout the house.

Or, if a large number show up, you might assign 2-3 people to a room, to pray over that room and the activities that take place there as they are led by the Holy Spirit.

If you are comfortable with anointing oil, anoint the doorframes, the windows, and the furniture as well, asking for God's protection and blessing.

Return to the main room for a closing prayer (add songs if you'd like!), joining hands in a circle. (Or use the Candle-Lighting Ceremony on page 61.)

And then . . . *eat* of course! Can be as simple as finger foods and cold or hot drinks, or as zesty as hot wings, served with celery sticks and ranch dressing (though you'll need *lots* of napkins and cold water to drink!).

Scriptures to Use

Choose from the following Scriptures to be read by various friends, family members, or your pastor as you go from room to room, followed by a prayer:

- ***The first blessing:*** "Grace and peace to [this house] from God our Father and the

Lord Jesus Christ" (Romans 1:7b, NIV).

- ***The front door:*** "Jesus said, 'Here I am! I stand at the door and knock. If anyone hears my voice and opens the door, I will come in . . ." (Revelation 3:20, NIV). *Sample prayer:* "Lord, we invite You into this home, to be Lord of all that is said and done within these walls, because we know that . . ." *Read the following Scripture:* "Unless the Lord builds the house, the builders labor in vain" (Psalm 127:1a, NIV).
- ***Blessing the "living areas" with their books, music, magazines, and TV:*** "By wisdom a house is built, and through understanding it is established; through knowledge its rooms are filled with all rare and beautiful treasures" (Proverbs 24:3-4, NIV). *Sample prayer:* "Lord, we dedicate our reading, our listening, our viewing, and even our conversations to You, that we might grow in Your wisdom and Your knowledge. Thank You for books and music, for radio and TV, for all the information available to us and the entertainment we enjoy. Help us to use it wisely and for Your glory."
- ***Blessing the kitchen and dining room:*** "A [family] can do nothing better than to eat and drink and find satisfaction in [their] work. This too, I see, is from the hand of God, for without him, who can eat or find enjoyment?" (Ecclesiastes 2:24, 25, NIV). *Sample prayer:* "Lord, bless the hands that prepare food in this house. Give us a thankful spirit for Your daily provision of food, never taking it for granted. Help us to slow down long enough to eat together as a family, enjoying one another around this table—and help us all to share the burden of washing dishes and cleaning up."
- ***Blessing the bedrooms:*** "There remains, then, a Sabbath-rest for the people of God; for anyone who enters God's rest also rests from his [or her] own work, just as God did from his" (Hebrews 4:10, NIV). *Sample prayer:* "Lord, give sweet rest within this room, the renewal of the mind, body, and spirit through sufficient sleep, to prepare [occupant name or names] for each new day."
- ***Blessing a child's room:*** "Jesus said, 'Let the children come to me. Do not stop them! For the kingdom of God belongs to such as these.' And he put his hands on their heads and blessed them . . ." (Matthew 19:14, 15, NLT). *Sample prayer:* Lord, as Jesus did, we bless [child's name]. Send Your guardian angel to protect [child's name] at home, and also at school and in the neighborhood. May [child's name] fall asleep each night, free from fear and scary dreams."
- ***Blessing the guest room and/or the family table:*** "Do not neglect to show hospitality to strangers, for thereby some have

entertained angels unawares" (Hebrews 13:2, NASB). *Also,* "Then the King will say to those on the right, 'Come, you who are blessed by my Father, inherit the Kingdom prepared for you from the foundation of the world. For I was hungry, and you fed me. I was thirsty, and you gave me a drink. I was a stranger, and you invited me into your home' . . . Then these righteous ones will reply, 'Lord, when did we ever see you . . . a stranger and show you hospitality?' . . . And the King will tell them, 'I assure you, when you did it to one of the least of these my brothers and sisters, you were doing it to me!'" (Matthew 25:34-40, NLT). *Sample prayer:* "Lord, give us the privilege of hospitality, of inviting both friends and strangers to share our table. Give us a generous spirit, Lord, sharing the blessing of this home with others, and may they find Your Spirit around our table and in this guest room."

- ***The Family Bible:*** "These commandments that I give you today are to be upon your hearts. Impress them on your children. Talk about them when you sit at home and when you walk along the road, when you lie down and when you get up" (Deuteronomy 6:6. 7, NIV). *Sample prayer:* "Lord, this Bible contains the living Word of God. Don't let it collect dust in this home. We dedicate ourselves to read it together as a family, to teach our children its precepts, and to be examples to them by obeying Your commandments—especially the two most important commandments to love God with all our heart, soul, and mind, and to love our neighbor as ourselves."

Candle-Lighting Ceremony

A simple candle-lighting ceremony might be another way to dedicate a home—either used by itself or to close the House Blessing.

Arrange eight candles on the dining room table. Ahead of time, write each of the following words that are in CAPITAL LETTERS on a small folded card (so it can stand up like a place card), and put the cards in a basket. As family and friends gather around the table, ask different ones to draw a card from the basket, set it in front of a candle, and then light a candle for each word. *Option:* Invite family and friends to add comments or prayers as each candle is lit.

We dedicate this home to JESUS.
We dedicate this home to LOVE.
We dedicate this home to JOY.
We dedicate this home to HOSPITALITY.
We dedicate this home to COOPERATION.
We dedicate this home to APPRECIATION.
We dedicate this home to
SPIRITUAL NURTURING.
We dedicate this home to
CHRISTIAN SERVICE.

(Feel free to add others prayers if you'd like—just be sure to provide more candles!

A Prayer from the Author of This Book:

Lord, bless the homes that will be blessed because someone reads the ideas here in this book. Oh, God, pour out Your Spirit in power upon the family in each home. Protect them from all harm and danger. Fill their homes with love and laughter, order and discipline, rest and renewal. Provide for every daily need. And give each family thankful hearts, for we know that the source of all that is good comes from You. Amen.

Hospital Hospitality

The wonderful thing about a prayer group of Yada Yada sisters who come from different Christian traditions and cultural backgrounds—whether fictional, as the sisters in *The Yada Yada Prayer Group*, or a group of real-life sisters-in-Christ (maybe like yours!)—is that we can share the rich rituals and celebrations that come from our various spiritual and family heritages.

And then there are times when we simply have to create our own traditions and celebrations! Even during the tough times. Maybe especially during the tough times.

The Phone Rings . . .

. . . A friend or family member has had an accident, is suddenly ill, or scheduled for surgery. You pop in during visiting hours and bring a card or some flowers, and like a good guest, you don't stay too long.

But hospital stays can be as exhausting for the family as for the patient. Long hours at the hospital. Lost hours of sleep. Cafeteria food. The nurses and doctors are taking care of the patient—but who's taking care of the family caregivers?

And as you probably know, being the *patient* isn't exactly the funnest way to spend a perfectly good week of your life.

But with a little thought and putting heads together with friends, there are a number of ways to make a hospital stay a bit less fearful, a bit less frazzled, a bit less lonely, a bit less unhealthy for *both* the patient and his or her family.

Hospital Guest Book

- Purchase a simple notebook with lined pages. (If you use an actual guestbook, be sure it has space for visitors to write notes, not just space for name and address.)
- Make a "title page" on the cover or first page, using colored markers, stickers, or fun fonts on your computer. (E.g. One ten-year-old decorated the notebook cover and titled it: "Grandpa's

Hospital Guest Book.")

- Write "Date & Time" on the top left of each page, followed by "Name & Notes."
- Encourage each person who comes to the waiting room during surgery and recovery—when the patient is decidedly "out of it"—to write notes of greeting, good wishes, and prayers in the guest book.
- Keep the book going with visitors who come each day: pastor, in-laws, buddies, kids, grandkids. If a visitor comes when the patient is asleep or out for testing, the patient will still be able to know who came to visit.
- The book can also be used as a "log" by the spouse or primary caregiver of progress each day, feelings, and things said that might be forgotten.
- The Hospital Guest Book will be a treasure to read and re-read once the patient is home and recovering.

Care for the Caregiver

Family members aren't always prepared for a hospital stay, especially in an emergency. Here are some things you can do . . .

- Bring a pillow and light blanket for those long nights in a waiting room.
- Bring some healthy snacks: small bottles of orange juice, fruit, nuts, granola bars, even some raw veggies. And replenish those snacks from time to time.
- Offer to go to the home and pick up their toothbrush, toilet kit, shaver—whatever will make them feel human after a long day and night at the hospital.
- Once the patient is back in the hospital room, offer to sit with him or her to give the spouse or caregiver time to go home for a shower or get out for a walk.
- Ask if plants at home need to be watered, kitty litter scooped, or the dog walked.

Cheer for the Patient

- Print out the patient's favorite Scriptures in large letters on colorful 8" x 10" paper and tape them around the hospital room. Or even just words of encouragement: "God Loves You" . . . "This Is the Day the Lord Has Made" . . . "God Is Your Rock." (You'll often find that the nurses and cleaning staff are encouraged, too!)
- Bring a small, portable CD player and some of the patient's favorite worship CDs for those long hours when he or she needs encouragement and comfort.
- If you bring cut flowers, be sure you also bring a vase to put them in! (The nurses might throw a conniption if you try to use the plastic water pitcher!)
- A basket to hold Get Well cards will be

appreciated. (Space to display cards is limited in a hospital room.)

Once the Patient is Home

- Arrange for a week's worth of meals to be brought in by friends, church members, neighbors. Disposable containers are best, so the patient's family doesn't have to return a stack of dishes to half a dozen different folks—but if that's not possible, make sure each "angel" clearly labels his or her dishes. And *you* offer to return them.
- Again, offer to "patient sit," so the family caregiver can get out to do errands, go for a walk, go to church Sunday morning, even take in a movie.
- A cleaning crew might be appreciated to do a once-over of the house: bathrooms, kitchen floor, vacuuming. One hour by a few good friends can certainly give a house or an apartment a quick but much-needed face-lift.

You get the idea! You'll probably think of other gifts of hospitality specific to your relative's or friend's situation. And don't think you have to do all the above by yourself. That's where you "yada yada" with your prayer sisters and spread the care and the cheer around.

Who knows, next time the patient might be you.

Family Reunions

Ever been in an airport—or at a hotel, or in a park—and seen dozens of people wearing the exact same T-shirt? Your first thought: sports team! But then you realize the T-shirt wearers range in age from toddlers in diapers to toddling elders pushing walkers, funky teenagers to stylish professionals, adults of all shapes and sizes, and kids. Lots of kids. It can mean only one thing …

A family reunion!

Family reunions give extended family members, often scattered among different cities and states—or even coast to coast—a chance to reconnect with and celebrate that all-important social construct: the *family.* To give younger generations a chance to hear stories from older generations before those stories are lost. To learn about one's family history. Maybe even discover cousins you didn't know you had! And most of all, to set aside some time in our hectic lives to simply enjoy each other.

Family reunions can be found across all social and economic classes and ethnic groups, as well as in many countries. But family reunions have special meaning and play an important role for African Americans in the United States.

Black Family Reunions

The history of black families in the United

States is a painful one. Ripped from their roots in Africa and sold into slavery, some survived the horrors of the sea voyage only to see their families torn apart on the auction block, mothers screaming as their husbands and children were sold separately, never to see them again.

With the Emancipation Proclamation, many African Americans made a concerted effort to find and reunite with family members, though the success rate was tragically low. Even after "freedom," grinding poverty, Jim Crow Laws, and debilitating discrimination drove many families to move out of the south, even if it meant leaving extended family members behind.

And yet . . . the black family endured. When *Roots,* by Alex Haley, was published in 1976, many African Americans were motivated to discover their own roots. During slavery, official birth certificates were rarely recorded, so a lot of family history and traditions were handed down orally . . . or kept surreptitiously in the family Bible by those who could read and write, and carefully passed down from generation to generation. Even records of slave sales and ship manifests helped some trace their ancestors.

Once found or re-established, it became crucially important to hold on to these family ties. Many black family reunions are large, including third and fourth cousins or great-uncles twice-removed. It takes a dedicated person within the family to keep track of the genealogical data.

Another gift of the African American family has been the black church, which in countless ways has *been* "family" in the African American community since slavery times, keeping the bond of family together both physically and spiritually.

Pulling It Together

Whatever your ethnic or cultural background, family reunions can be an anchor in our increasingly fragmented day and age. And here are some ideas how to pull a Family Reunion together:

First Things First

There are six things that determine everything else related to planning a family reunion:

(1) **Reunion Coordinator or Committee.** A successful reunion can use many volunteers, talents, and skills. But you *do* need someone or a small committee of 3-4 to get things rolling and keep things on schedule.

(2) **Date.** Set the date the previous year—9 to 12 months is a good target to get your chosen date on the calendar *and* choose a place, especially if you need to make reservations for a destination reunion. Actual planning for activities should begin 6 months in advance.

(3) **Location.** Will it be . . . local? Held at a park, a community center, a church?

Or a destination reunion?—held at a resort (like Disney World or a Dude Ranch), at a hotel in a major city, or even a camp or retreat center?

Reserve the location!

(4) **Size.** Reunions can be "small"—maybe just Grandma and Grandpa, their children, and their grandchildren and great-grands. (Though even "small" can end up being fairly large!)

Or "large." A reunion can include the extended family—aunts, uncles, and cousins, or even great-aunts and uncles, second- and third-cousins and once or twice-removed—possibly running into the hundreds.

The size, of course, will help determine the location . . . and so it goes.

(5) **Accommodations.** If invitees are mostly local, family members can sleep at home and all convene at a local park or community center for the festivities.

If a significant number of people travel, consideration must be given to where people can stay. For some reunions, everyone might stay at the same hotel or resort or retreat center. For others, you may need to provide a list of hotels/motels for people traveling which they obtain on their own.

(6) **Meeting space.** Consideration must be given to where events and activities will take place. This, of course, will depend on the kind of events and activities that the Activity Committee plans (see below). You will usually need a combination for different kinds of events: a park for outdoor play or sports, a large meeting room for indoor events (hotel meeting room? school gym? church fellowship room?), a restaurant or banquet facility or hotel ballroom for your special banquet, and/or a variety of nearby cafes and restaurants for those "meals on your own."

Once you've decided the basics—coordinator(s), date, location, size, accommodations, and meeting space—get other family members involved, using the energy, creativity, and talents of young and old to plan some of the following:

Communication

- What's the best way to communicate with your family members? Facebook group? Email? Mailed flyers? A combination?
- Choose someone (ideally a person on the coordinating committee who knows the latest info, but could be someone else) who is *good* at communication—i.e., someone who can be counted on to send pertinent info to attendees on a regular basis—at least every month to begin,

then every week as you get close.
- **Update** everyone's contact info *at* the reunion—print out what you have, let people correct it and/or add any new information. (Emails, phone numbers, and addresses often change. Add new babies and new spouses!) This will be your contact list for the *next* reunion!

Treasurer and Registration

- Depending on the type of reunion you have, you need to decide how to cover the costs for accommodations, activities, and reserving event spaces.
- In order to share the expenses equitably, individuals and families should *register* their intention to attend 6 months in advance. You could ask for an initial *reservation fee*, with the remainder to be determined once you know what the actual expenses will be and how many plan to attend.
- Travel *to* the reunion is generally up to the individual person or family.

T-Shirts

- Reunion T-shirts are part of the fun (and make it easier to keep track of kids if you're at the zoo or a theme park or in a crowd!). Enlist a creative volunteer to take care of designing, ordering, and delivering T-shirts
- There are many different online companies who can help you design your reunion T-shirt. Just type "Family Reunion T-Shirts" into your browser (e.g. Google) and choose one that fits your budget and style.
- Be sure your design includes your family name *and* the date! (Example: BROWN FAMILY REUNION, July XX, 2020.) You can also add the location (E.g. YMCA Camp of the Rockies).
- Once you've chosen your T-shirt style, include the price of the T-shirt in your registration fee, and a place for each family member to choose the SIZE they want.
- Your T-shirts can be all the same color & design OR different colors for different family groups.
- Family members will pick up their T-shirts when they arrive at the reunion.

Name Tags

- If your family is large, you might also want to have *name tags* at the actual reunion, to help people "remember" who's who!

Food

- Whether your reunion is one day or a long weekend, small or large, *food* is essential to a successful family reunion. "Breaking bread" together around the table is the essence of family and fellowship.
- If most people live nearby or within a short driving distance, a *potluck* (or *pot blessing* as it's known in some circles) for one of the main meals is both fun and a

chance to show off traditional ethnic foods or favorite recipes handed down through generations. A fun twist: encourage cooks to print up copies of their special recipe to pass on to other family members!

- One way to ensure you don't end up with everyone bringing desserts (!) is to assign food groups alphabetically. For example: A-D Appetizers, E-I Salads, J-P Main Dishes, Q-T Desserts, U-Z Drinks . . or however your family names tend to fall along the alphabet.
- If your *potluck* is outside, of course, it becomes a *barbeque* or *picnic*! An evening picnic can include a *bonfire* with hot dogs over the fire, followed by yummy, sticky *s'mores.*
- If most people travel to the reunion and can't bring food, you can (a) reserve a party room at a restaurant or at the hotel, or (b) engage a caterer for your Big Night. People are then "on your own" for other meals.
- If you are at a retreat center or camp where you need to prepare *all* the meals, you might assign certain meals (or days) to certain families to provide/cook/clean-up. This works well with groups of 20-30.

Auction

Want to raise money toward the next reunion?

- Do you have a special family project or charity or family foundation? Have an AUCTION!
- Bid for family memorabilia (embroidered table runners, great-grandma's doll, hand-crocheted afghan, set of china, great-aunt's jewelry, etc.)
- Bid for "services"—cut grass, wash windows, homemade pie, half hour massage, driving lesson for a teen, knitting or cooking lesson, etc.
- Bid for crafts made by family members—macramé plant hangers, a painting, pottery, handmade aprons or doll clothes, jewelry, etc.

Activities (NOTE: Each activity needs its own coordinator***)***

- **Talent Show Night**

  Invite all kinds of talent: dance (modern, ballet, tap, breakdance!), playing instruments, singing, telling family stories, juggling, rapping, stand-up comedy, magic tricks . . . a guaranteed fun evening!
- **Slide Show of Family Photos**

  Photos can be sent digitally and put together on a CD. (Then the person putting it together doesn't have to return photos!)

  A Slide Show is excellent entertainment shown on Banquet or night.
- **Fun Family Fotos**

  Provide a colorful backdrop, provide dress-ups (silly hats, stoles, funny glasses, costume jewelry, old-fashioned clothes, whatever!) and take a fun/funny family photo of each family group!

Someone could make this into a photo book or photo calendar that people can order as a souvenir of the reunion!

- **Outdoor Sports**

  Softball, volleyball, flag football
- **Multi-Generational Outdoor Games.**

  Bean bag toss
  Washers (similar to Bean Bag toss)
  Ladder ball (Blongo Ball)
  Bocce Ball
  Croquet
  Sack races, relays
- **Indoor: Board games, card games**

  Apples to Apples
  Bananagrams
  Bid Whist
  Hoopla!
  Settlers of Catan
  Spoons (card game)
  Ticket to Ride
  UNO
- **Sightseeing Tours of Host City**

  On one day, plan a trip to the zoo, a museum, Six Flags, botanic gardens or conservatory, bus tours, boat tour, etc.
- **Worship Service**

  If the majority of your family are people of faith, a worship service together is entirely appropriate, and can be a meaningful way to end your reunion.

  Could be a nighttime "fireside" if you're at a retreat center or camp. Or if your reunion is on a weekend, Sunday morning is a natural time for a short time of worship together.

  But be sure it's kid friendly!

  Sing! (Provide song sheets?) Depending on your mix of relatives, you might want to include a variety of songs: Gospel, hymns, praise-and-worship contemporary songs. A keyboard helps! Or put together a praise band!

  A short play from the Bible done by the kids would be enjoyed by everyone!

  Close with a short devotional by an aspiring pastor or by the matriarch or patriarch of the family.

  Last but never least, PRAY for one another. This might include the older generation(s) giving a blessing to each person of the younger generations. (See "Naming and Blessing" on page 46.)

Got enough ideas for your next Family Reunion? Simple or elaborate, one day or several, your family will remember your reunion for many years to come. It's worth the sweat!

Starting a Yada Yada Prayer Group

Is God tugging at your heart to start a prayer group? But you feel totally inadequate? God will give you wisdom, sister! (Read James 1:5 and *ask*!) There is no one-size-fits-all formula for putting together a prayer group, but here are a few things to consider:

Prepare Yourself . . .

First of all, bring your desire to God and pray about it! (Funny how often we skip this step.)

Ask another sister to pray with you. "If two of you agree . . . about anything they ask for, it will be done for them" (Matthew 18:19, NIV).

Read *The Power of Praying Together* by Stormie Omartian (Harvest House). This sister knows what she's talking about!

Then . . .

Share with your pastor what you want to do. Choose a time for your prayer group to meet that does not conflict with other church meetings or responsibilities.

Who needs it? A prayer group for women in your church is perfectly legitimate. (Many "church" women are lonely or alone.) OR maybe God is calling you to reach beyond your circle of friends—to neighbors, co-workers, another parent at your child's school, across cultural or racial boundaries. This takes prayer and intentionality.

Personally invite other sisters to join you. If two of you are in agreement about starting a prayer group, each of you could invite one more. That's four. Then those four each invite one. That's eight. A good beginning!

Meet in your home—or ask another sister to host. Or share hosting among all the members of the prayer group. Meeting in homes helps create a circle of intimacy. Also, women who are not members of your church may feel more comfortable coming to a home meeting. (But if God directs you to meet at the office, at the park, at a coffee shop, at the jail, or at the church—do it!)

Size? Don't let the group get too big. Twelve is usually a maximum for a small group. Eight to ten is a good number. (If lots of women want to become a part, you may need to divide into two groups! What a wonderful "problem" to have.)

Leaders: Be sure one or two of the sisters who are well grounded in the Word of God are willing to function as leaders/facilitators.

The Meeting Itself . . .

Fellowship. Allow at least fifteen minutes for women to arrive, get snacks or drinks, and "unwind."

Begin with worship—a Scripture, a song, prayers of praise—to get your focus where it needs to be, on God alone.

Study the Word. Spend time in the Word. This can either be a Bible study using a study guide, a book study from the Bible itself (e.g., the Gospel of John, the Epistle of James etc.), or a short devotion from the Word taught by someone in the group. But you will need someone to facilitate so you *do* leave time to . . .

PRAY! Share brief prayer requests. This is not the time for lengthy sharing or giving advice. Don't just talk about what needs prayer. *Pray* for one another!

Respect! Agree together that personal things shared in the group are to remain in the group—not fodder for gossip. (However, if things come up that are too big to handle in the group, the leaders may need to seek outside counsel.)

Last but not Least . . .

Pray during the week for the women who attend the group. Call to check on anyone who is missing, and pray for them over the phone.

Be expectant that God can do great things in you and through you as you pray.

Section 3

Recipes from Book One

About the book:

What do an ex-con, a former drug addict, a real estate broker, a college student, and a married mother of two have in common? Nothing, or so Jodi Baxter thought.

From Jodi's Journal: "I almost didn't go to that Chicago Women's Conference—after all, being thrown together with five hundred strangers wasn't exactly my 'comfort zone.' But I would be rooming with my boss, Avis, and I hoped to make a friend or two.

"When Avis and I were assigned to a prayer group of twelve women at the conference, I wasn't sure what to think. There was Flo, an outspoken ex-drug addict; Ruth, a Messianic Jew who could smother-mother you to death; and Yo-Yo, an ex-con who wasn't even a Christian! Not to mention women from Jamaica, Honduras, South Africa—practically a mini-United Nations. We certainly didn't have much in common.

"But something happened that weekend. Talk about a rock tumbler!—knocking off each other's rough edges, learning to laugh and cry together. But when I faced the biggest crisis of my life, God used my newfound girlfriends to help teach me—Jodi Baxter, longtime Christian 'good girl'—what it means to be just a sinner saved by grace."

But there's more!

Put twelve feisty women in one prayer group, ranging in age from twenty to fifty-something, add a variety of skin colors, cultural backgrounds, ethnic upbringings, and years of church potlucks . . . and what do you get?

Food!

To introduce our cast of Yada Yada characters, here are some "Signature Recipes" from each Yada Yada sister. "Signature?" you ask. Yep. Just another way of saying, if you see that on the potluck table, you know who made it without even seeing the name taped to the bowl (or pot, or plate, or whatever).

Jodi's No-Fail Chicken-and-Rice Casserole

Jodi Baxter's favorite when it comes to throwing stuff together for a church potluck or when she can't think of anything else to make for supper. No fail, too—IF she remembers to turn on the oven. Don't be a Jodi when it comes to little details like that.

1 chicken, cut up, or 8-10 pieces with skin on

3 cups rice

2 (10.5-oz.) cans cream of mushroom soup

3 soup cans water (or use part white wine)

2 packages dry onion soup mix

[Metric conversion chart on page 141]

1. Preheat oven to 350 degrees. Prepare 6-quart casserole by spraying with baking spray.

2. Mix cream of mushroom soup, water, and dry onion soup mix together. Pour a small amount in bottom of baking dish.

3. Measure raw rice into bottom of baking dish. Add half of soup & water mixture and moisten rice thoroughly. Arrange chicken pieces on top. Pour remaining soup & water mixture on top.

4. Cover. Place on middle rack in 350-degree oven for 1½ hours. Or bake at 325 degrees for 2½ to 3 hours.

The secret to this tasty casserole is cooking it long enough so that the rice is tender, but not letting it dry out. It helps if you remember to turn on the oven—but we already said that.

Full recipe serves 6-8 (half recipe serves 3-4).

Stu's Ramen Noodle Salad

What Stu brought to the Mother's Day Potluck at Uptown Community Church. (Good thing, since Jodi forgot to put her "no-fail" chicken-and-rice casserole into the oven.) Stu keeps stuff like dark sesame oil (has a lovely oriental nutty flavor), rice vinegar, and fresh gingerroot on hand, which might seem a bit much for the average household-with-kids, but she swears they make a world of difference for anything oriental—and salads.

1 package (4 oz.) ramen noodles (or use 4 oz. spaghetti, broken)

3 Tbsp. oil

3 Tbsp. honey

1 Tbsp. soy sauce

1 Tbsp. dark sesame oil

1 Tbsp. rice vinegar

1½ tsp. grated gingerroot

1 tsp. crushed red pepper flakes

3 cups cooked chicken, chilled and shredded

1 cup finely shredded red cabbage

4 green onions, sliced thin

2 large carrots, shredded

1 red bell pepper, sliced into thin strips or chopped

½ cup dry-roasted peanuts

1. Cook the ramen noodles as directed on the package. (Or cook spaghetti to *al dente.*)

2. *For dressing:* Combine oil, honey, soy sauce, dark sesame oil, rice vinegar, gingerroot, and red pepper flakes in a small bowl and whisk thoroughly.

3. Shred chicken and chop vegetables; set aside.

4. Drain noodles and rinse with cold water. Then, in a large bowl, combine noodles, chicken, and vegetables. Toss with dressing. Top with peanuts (or pass separately).

Serves 6.

Avis's Deluxe Macaroni and Cheese

Avis modestly says "mac-and-cheese" is one of the few things she can cook. "Everything else turns out raw or charred." Only later did the Yada Yadas discover this is actually true! As far as they're concerned, she can stick with the "mac-and-cheese." It's good!

2 cups elbow macaroni, cooked and drained according to package directions

¼ cup butter or margarine

¼ cup flour

1 tsp. powdered mustard

2½ cups milk

3 cups coarsely shredded sharp cheddar cheese

¼ tsp. salt

¼ tsp. fresh ground pepper

1 Tbsp. Worcestershire sauce

Tabasco sauce to taste (3 good shots)

Paprika as desired

1. Preheat oven to 350 degrees.
2. While macaroni is cooking, melt butter in saucepan over moderate heat. Blend in flour and dry mustard. Slowly whisk in milk. Cook, whisking, until thickened. Mix in 2 cups of cheese and remaining ingredients *except* macaroni. Cook and stir until cheese melts.
3. Remove cheese mixture from heat; mix in macaroni. Turn mixture into a buttered 2-qt. casserole dish. Sprinkle with remaining 1 cup of cheese. Sprinkle with paprika as desired. Bake, uncovered, for 30 minutes until bubbly and lightly browned.

Serves 6, more or less.

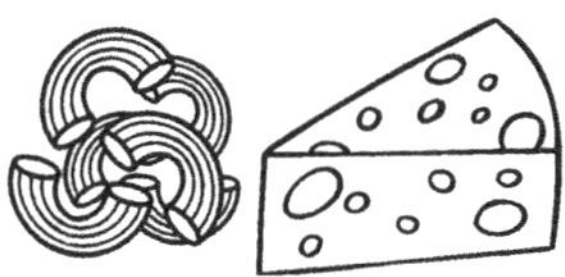

Florida's Quick Catfish Dinner

Who has time to spend an hour in the kitchen? Not Florida! When she gets home from work, not only are the husband and kids clamoring for supper, her own stomach is growling. Good thing about catfish—it cooks up in a jiffy. Good, too.

4 catfish fillets, about 2 lbs.

½ cup Italian-seasoned bread crumbs

2 Tbsp. flour

½ tsp. seasoned salt

4 Tbsp. butter or corn oil

Fresh parsley

Louisiana or Tabasco hot sauce

Also . . .

1½ cups white rice

1 pkg. frozen green peas

1. Put rice, 3 cups of water, and 1 tsp. salt in a saucepan, cover, and bring to boil, then turn heat down to a low simmer for 12 minutes.

2. Throw frozen peas in a saucepan with 1 cup of water and bring to a slow boil.

3. While rice and peas are cooking, heat butter or oil in a skillet large enough to accommodate the catfish fillets. Put the bread crumbs, flour, and seasoning in a paper bag, lunch size. Drop in fillets and shake two or three times until each fillet is coated. (Too much shaking will break up fillets.) Place the fillets in the hot skillet and cook on a medium-high heat for about 5-7 minutes per side until golden brown.

4. Serve with rice and peas, which should be done about the time the fillets are golden brown. Garnish the catfish with fresh parsley sprigs and provide hot sauce for those who want it.

Serves 4.

Chanda's Jamaican Rice and Peas

"Why you need a recipe?" Chanda scoffs, when asked about her favorite recipe for Jamaican Rice and Peas. "Just cook up some red peas, t'row in spices and coconut milk and some rice. What's so 'ard about dat?"

Well, fine. But just in case you need a little help, here are a few tips from Chanda.

1½ cups *cooked* red kidney beans, reserving cooking liquid

1 clove garlic, chopped

1¼ cups unsweetened coconut milk, *plus . . .*

Reserved bean liquid and enough water to make 2¼ cups combined liquid

1 cup rice

2 green onions, chopped (*or* 1 med. onion, chopped)

1 or 2 sprigs fresh thyme (or ½ tsp. dried thyme)

Salt and pepper to taste

1. Dried red beans are the "peas" in Jamaican Rice and Peas, though fresh Pigeon peas (Gungo peas) are used in season. **Cooking dried beans:** Soak beans overnight in plenty of water, *or* (quick method) put dried beans in a pot, add water (about 2 inches above beans), bring to a boil for one minute, turn off stove, cover pot, and let sit for one hour. Then gently simmer soaked beans until tender.

2. Put *cooked* red beans into a large pot. Add garlic. Measure all liquids (coconut milk, reserved bean liquid, and water) to make 2¼ cups, and add to the pot. Add rice, onion, and seasonings. Bring to a boil, reduce heat, cover, and simmer for 20 to 30 minutes or until all liquid is absorbed.

Note: If using canned beans, drain, but save liquid to add to the coconut milk and water. Then simply add the canned beans to the pot with the rice.

Serves 4-6.

Ruth's Cheese Blintzes

Cheese blintzes are traditional fare for Shavuot—the Jewish Feast of Weeks, otherwise known as Pentecost. The first time Ruth made these yummy delicacies for her Yada Yada sisters, Yo-Yo piped up, "Why don't they just call 'em cottage cheese pancakes and be done with it?" . . . which earned her a whole string of Yiddishisms we can't repeat here.

Batter:

4 eggs

1 cup milk (or ½ cup milk and ½ cup water)

1 cup flour

¼ cup sugar

⅛ tsp. salt

2 Tbsp. oil or melted butter

Filling:

1 pound cottage cheese (dry type, or strained)

2 beaten eggs

2 Tbsp. flour

2 Tbsp. sugar

1 tsp. vanilla

Continued on next page

Making the Crepes:

1. Combine batter ingredients until smooth (use mixer, blender, or food processor).
2. Heat a small frying pan (about 7 inches)—non-stick or a heavy, seasoned pan works best—with a small amount of oil or spray with cooking spray.
3. Pour ⅓ cup batter into hot pan and tip frying pan to spread batter around evenly. Cook briefly until small air bubbles form; bottom should be golden brown.
4. Turn over and allow to cook another 5 seconds.
5. Remove crepe to a plate.
6. Stack warm crepes between sheets of wax paper so they don't stick.

Filling the Crepes:

1. Combine ingredients for filling; mix well.
2. Place a heaping tablespoon of filling along one side of each crepe.

3. Fold over once to cover filling, then tuck in sides and finish rolling.

4. Set aside until all crepes are filled. Now they're blintzes!

Frying the Blintzes:

1. Melt 1 Tbsp. butter in frying pan.

2. Add three blintzes at a time, turning once until both sides are golden brown and crisp.

Baking the Blintzes:

1. Preheat oven to 350 degrees.

2. Lightly grease a 9 x 13-inch pan and line up the blintzes.

3. Prepare topping by beating sour cream and eggs together until thick and creamy.

4. Add remaining ingredients and beat well.

5. Pour topping over the blintzes and bake 1 hour.

Serving the Blintzes:

1. Serve hot with fresh cut-up fruit, such as peaches, strawberries, blueberries, or etc. Or puree frozen berries and serve as a sauce. Allow 2-3 blintzes per serving. (Go ahead, *nosh* away!)

Makes 16-18 blintzes.

Topping:

2 cups sour cream (can use half yogurt)

6 eggs

1 tsp. vanilla

1 tsp. cornstarch

¼ tsp. salt

Plus . . .

¼ cup melted butter (or oil) for frying blintzes

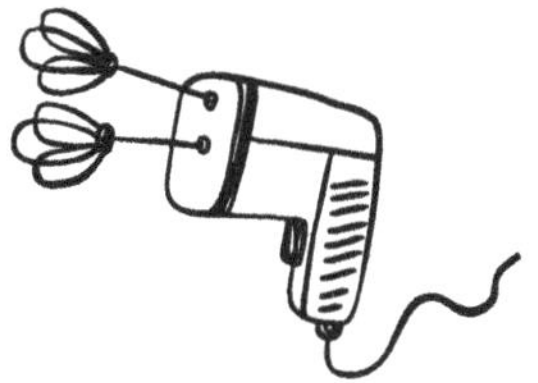

Yo-Yo's Brothers' PB&Js

Cook?" Yo-Yo says. "What for? Don't matter what I make; my brothers just want peanut-butter and jelly. So, hey, I let 'em make their own PB&Js. It's food, ain't it?"

2 slices white bread (preferably the cheap kind that wads into a ball instead of crumbles)

Brand-name creamy peanut butter (forget "natural" peanut butter)

Jar of strawberry jam

Teen male version:

1. Dig knife into peanut butter and swab one slice of bread with thick layer of peanut butter.

2. Dig same knife into jar of strawberry jam; swab the other slice of bread with thick layer of jam.

3. Slap the two slices of bread together (peanut butter and jam on the *inside*).

4. Tell someone you're going "out" while your mouth is full of PB&J.

5. Leave jars of peanut butter and jam open on counter, along with gooey knife for someone else to clean up.

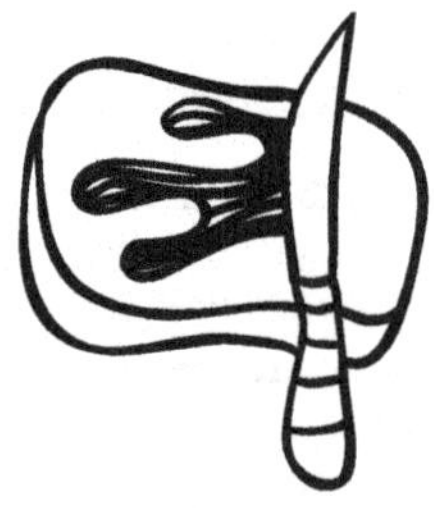

Adele's Foot-Stompin' Greens

Why "foot-stompin'"? Because when you take a forkful of Adele's greens, you want to stomp your feet and shout, "Hallelujah!" But you can't shout, because your mouth is full, so . . . foot stompin' will have to do to show just how mm-mm good these greens are.

2-3 lbs. collard greens (may substitute mustard or turnip greens)

1 pound smoked neck bone, ham hocks, or in a pinch ½ pound bacon fried not too crispy

2 medium onions, chopped

5 cloves of garlic, finely diced

1 tsp. crushed red pepper flakes

2 Tbsp. chicken bouillon

2 Tbsp. brown sugar

Note: Greens are easy to grow. Even a small patch in your yard will provide enough for you and your kin. Started early, they will be ready by late June, even in Chicago, and produce sometimes into December, tasting even better after the first freeze if it's not too hard.

1. Wash the greens and slice out the stem and central rib.
2. Stack several leaves on top of each other and roll them into a tube, then slice the roll to create ½ inch strips.
3. Put 1 inch of water in the bottom of a 6-8 qt. kettle and add all ingredients. Cover and bring to a boil.
4. Simmer 1- 2 hours or until the meat falls off the bones and the greens are tender, checking periodically that the liquid does not boil away. (Fresh greens will contribute liquid, but you don't want so much "pot likker" that the greens are floating in soup.)

Good any ol' time—but absolutely kickin' when served with cornbread, black eyed peas, and fried chicken!

Serves 6-8.

Delores's Mexicali Soup

Delores calls this soup "Mexicali," because it's a blend of Mexico and California, just like the capital of Baja California, Mexico, just "south of the border." (The Enriquez kids, however, call it "Taco Soup"!)

1. Fry together in large soup pot: ground beef, onion, and garlic until beef is no longer pink. Add taco seasoning; stir until well blended. Add cans: corn, pinto beans, black beans, green chilies, diced tomatoes, and broth.
2. Bring to a boil, reduce heat, cover, and simmer for 10-15 minutes.
3. When ready to serve, stir in lime juice and cilantro.
4. Ladle into bowls. Let your *niños* choose their garnish.

Serves 6.

1 pound lean ground beef

1 onion, chopped

3 garlic cloves, chopped or minced

1 package taco seasoning

1 (14.5 oz.) can corn

1 (14.5 oz.) can pinto beans (drained)

1 (14.5 oz.) can black beans (drained)

1 (6 oz.) can chopped green chilles (mild or hot, depending on taste)

2 (14.5 oz.) cans diced tomatoes—or 1 (28 oz.) can

2 (14.5 oz.) cans chicken broth (or equivalent water & chicken bouillion)

½ cup cilantro, chopped

3 limes, squeezed

Garnish: Shredded cheese; corn chips; sour cream

Nony's Swazi Butternut Soup

If you're lucky enough to get invited to the Sisulu-Smith household for dinner, don't be surprised if you're served this rich, golden, satisfying soup for the first course, a favorite South African starter to a meal of roast beef or lamb. But why wait for an invitation! Make this for your own family—and be prepared to offer seconds.

2 medium onions, chopped

4 Tbsp. butter or margarine

2 medium butternut squash, peeled, deseeded, and cut into cubes

1 large apple, peeled, cored, and chopped

1¼ tsp. curry powder

4 Tbsp. flour

½ tsp. ground nutmeg

3 cups chicken stock (homemade, canned, or water & chicken bouillion)

2 cups milk

1½ tsp. salt

Garnish: Parsley (chopped), sour cream

1. In a large saucepan or soup pot, sauté the chopped onions in the butter or margarine. Add chopped butternut, apple, and curry powder, continue to sauté gently. Add flour and nutmeg; stir until blended.

2. Now add chicken stock, milk, and salt to the vegetable mixture. Cover, bring to a boil, and continue cooking over medium heat until butternut pieces are soft, stirring occasionally.

3. Puree entire mixture (you may have to do 4 cups at a time) in a blender or food processor until soup is smooth and creamy.

4. Reheat and serve hot with a dollop of sour cream and sprinkles of chopped parsley.

Serves 6.

Edesa's Mama's Mango Salsa

Say "salsa" . . . think "tomato-salsa-in-a-jar"? Not if you drop by Edesa's apartment for a snack! Hondurans make good use of luscious mangoes growing everywhere in their country. Fortunately for us gringos, mangoes are becoming more common in the fruit and produce section of many grocery stores.

1 mango, peeled and diced

2 avocados, peeled and chopped

1 tomato, diced into tiny pieces

¼ cup red onion, diced

1 red pepper, diced into tiny pieces

1 garlic clove, minced

Juice of 1 lime

1. Peel, chop, and dice away! Combine all ingredients in a bowl, let it sit for 20 minutes to mingle flavors (*or* cover with plastic wrap and refrigerate overnight to preserve flavor).

2. Serve with tortilla chips—and you better double the recipe next time!

Serves 6.

How to Cut a Mango

Try this: Mangos have a single large, flat seed inside that gives the mango a slightly flattened shape.

1. Stand the mango on end with the flat sides facing to either side. With a large, sharp knife cut one thick slice off one side of the mango. (Your slice should be thick enough so your knife just skims the side of the internal seed.)

2. Turn the mango 180 degrees and cut a second slice off the other side.

3. Lay one of the slices skin-side down on a cutting board and with the tip of your knife cut a crosshatch pattern (with approximately ½–inch squares) across the meat of the fruit only deep enough to just reach the skin.

4. With the fruit side facing away from you, place your thumbs in the center of the skin side and your fingertips holding the edge and press the center of the skin away from you to turn it "inside out" enough so it is flat.

5. Then press the slice flat, skin-side down, on the cutting board leaving the expanded "flower" of fruit cubes sticking up.

6. With your knife parallel to the board, slice away from you just above the skin, releasing all the little cubes of the fruit.

7. Repeat with the other slice of the fruit.

8. You may be able to get a few more bites of fruit by cutting the rim of skin off the fruit still attached to the seed and then cutting away that fruit.

Hoshi's Japanese Spring Rolls

Any kind of Asian cooking calls for some special ingredients, but you can often find them in the produce section or specialty aisle at your grocery store. If not, locate the closest Asian market. It's worth it—spring rolls are fun to make! (Shh, don't tell Hoshi, but when Jodi tried this recipe, she substituted regular ol' white button mushrooms for the shiitake mushrooms, and the spring rolls were still good, if not exactly authentic.)

4-5 dried shiitake mushrooms

⅓ pound ground pork

1 Tbsp. cornstarch

1 oz. *harusame* (bean starch noodles), or cellophane noodles

1 Tbsp. vegetable oil

1 tsp. grated ginger

1 cup bean sprouts

1 can bamboo shoots, chopped

⅔ cup chicken broth

Continued on next page

Advance preparation:

1. Soak shiitake mushrooms in water for 30 minutes to soften.

2. Sprinkle cornstarch over ground pork and stir in well.

3. Drop *harusame* or cellophane noodles in a pan of boiling water for 1 minute, then drain and cut into 3-inch lengths.

4. Drain mushrooms and cut into thin strips.

Prepare filling:

1. Heat oil in large frying pan, add grated ginger and sauté briefly. Add ground pork and fry until it loses its pink color; add mushrooms, bamboo shoots, and bean sprouts and sauté.

2. Then add chicken broth, sugar, soy sauce, sesame oil, sake (or rice vinegar-plus-sugar), and noodles to the pan.

3. Heat through until mixture simmers; then add mixture of water and cornstarch. Stir well. Scoop filling into a bowl and cool.

Wrapping the wrappers:

1. Spoon 1-2 Tbsp. filling on egg roll wrapper.

2. Fold one side of wrapper over filling to cover; then tuck both sides of the wrapper inward and finish rolling.

3. Seal the edge with the mixture of water and flour.

Frying the spring rolls:

1. Heat oil in a deep frying pan to 360 degrees.

2. Fry spring rolls, turning until all sides are golden brown.

3. Drain and serve with soy sauce mixed with chili oil for dipping in.

Serves 6.

1 tsp. sugar

1½ Tbsp. soy sauce

1 tsp. sesame oil

2 Tbsp. sake rice wine (or 2 Tbsp. rice vinegar with a little sugar)

1 Tbsp. water mixed with 1 Tbsp. cornstarch

10 to 20 egg roll wrappers

1 tsp. flour mixed with 1 Tbsp. water

Vegetable oil for frying

Recipes from Book Two

About the book:

A robbery, a lynching, and a mourning mother shake up the Yada Yadas. The prayer group seemed invincible—until tension and distrust shake its very foundations!

From Jodi's Journal: "I have never felt so violated! The Yada Yada Prayer Group was 'gettin' down' with God in prayer and praise one night when a heroin-crazed woman barged into my house, demanded our valuables, and threatened us with a ten-inch knife—a knife that drew blood.

"We wondered if we'd ever get back to normal after this terrifying experience. I assumed we would. After all, we'd started praying together at the Chicago Women's Conference last spring, and we'd been through a lot already as spiritual sisters. This was just one more hurdle to conquer, right?

"But then things really took a turn for the worse when grim accusations were made against my husband, Denny. Racial division, pain, and pride are tearing our close-knit group apart, and I'm not sure if we'll be able to survive the mess. Is true forgiveness possible—not just with these close friends . . . but also with our enemies?"

Later, a shocking confrontation in Jodi's third-grade classroom forced her to face her own accountability and learn what true forgiveness really is.

Whew!

But even in the midst of all that drama, the Yada Yada sisters took time to celebrate some of the Jewish festivals and Mexican Independence Day and even an alternative Halloween (see Section I of this book) . . . and all that celebrating was bound to make *everyone* hungry! So here the Yada Yadas offer up some more of their favorite recipes, from main dishes to desserts. But don't worry. You don't have to wait for a party to enjoy any of the following . . .

Edesa's Easy Enchiladas

Edesa's mother may have made authentic Honduran enchiladas back in Honduras, but Edesa prefers the Mexican type and isn't above using a few American shortcuts to make them quick and easy.

1 pound ground beef

1 medium onion, chopped

3-4 cloves garlic, diced

1 envelope (1.25 oz.) dry taco seasoning

1 can (4 oz.) black olives, sliced

1 can (16 oz.) ranch style refried beans

2 cans (10 oz. each) enchilada sauce

12 corn tortillas

8 oz. grated Monterey Jack cheese

Toppings:

3-4 green onions, chopped

Fresh cilantro

Sour cream

Your favorite hot sauce

1. Brown beef, onion, and garlic; add the taco seasoning according to instructions on package. Stir in the olives and refried beans; heat through.

2. Warm the enchilada sauce in a separate sauce pan and pour half of it into the bottom of a 9 x 13 in. baking dish.

3. Fill each tortilla with about four tablespoons of the beef and bean mixture and roll to close.

4. Arrange side by side in the baking dish and pour the remaining sauce over the enchiladas.

5. Sprinkle the cheese on top and bake in a 350-degree oven for about 30 minutes or until thoroughly heated.

6. Top with fresh cilantro, a dollop of sour cream, chopped green onion, and hot sauce to taste.

Serves 6.

Jodi's Pasta with Gorgonzola Cheese Sauce

Jodi found this recipe in a newspaper, clipped it, played around with the ingredients, and it quickly made its way onto the Baxter Five-Star Recipe list (very easy and very good!).

1 pound spaghetti or other pasta

1 medium red bell pepper, seeded and sliced into thin strips

1-2 cups small broccoli tips

3 Tbsp. extra virgin olive oil

8 oz. Gorgonzola cheese, crumbled

1 cup soymilk (or ½ cup each, milk and half-and-half)

½ cup grated Parmesan cheese

1. While cooking the spaghetti according to the directions on the package, sauté the red pepper in 1 tablespoon of olive oil and set aside.

2. Cook half the soymilk, all the Gorgonzola cheese, and the remaining olive oil in a sauce pan over a low heat, stirring constantly until the cheese melts. Add the remaining soymilk and heat.

3. Place the broccoli tips in the bottom of a bowl. Place a colander on top and drain the hot spaghetti into it. The boiling water will drain through and blanch the broccoli tips.

4. Place drained spaghetti in a warmed serving bowl.

5. Pour the cheese mixture over it. Scatter broccoli and red pepper on top and sprinkle with the Parmesan cheese.

Serve with garlic bread and a large green salad.

Serves 4-6.

Jodi's Red Velvet Cake

There are dozens of recipes for Red Velvet Cake, and some may be nearly as good as Jodi's with their signature hint of chocolate. But Jodi's real trick is the mock whipped cream frosting she lathers on it, setting off the rich, red cake like a soft, white, feather boa over a crimson velvet dress.

2 eggs

½ cup shortening

1½ cups sugar

½ tsp. salt

2 oz. red food coloring (e.g. two 1 oz. bottles)

2½ Tbsp. instant cocoa mix

1 Tbsp. vanilla

1 cup buttermilk

2 ½ cups flour

1 Tbsp. vinegar

1tsp. soda

Frosting:

1 cup milk

4½ Tbsp. flour

1½ sticks margarine (¾ cup)

4½ Tbsp. shortening

1½ cups sugar

1 Tbsp. vanilla

For the cake:

1. Mix the eggs, shortening, sugar, and salt. Add and mix in the food coloring, cocoa, and vanilla. Add alternately (a little of each at a time) the buttermilk and flour while continue to mix until smooth. Fold in the vinegar and soda.

2. Grease and flour three 8-inch or two 9-inch pans. Distribute the mix evenly in the pans and bake at 350 degrees for 30 minutes.

For the frosting:

1. In a saucepan whisk together the milk and flour and cook until thick, stirring frequently. Set aside until cool. (If necessary, you can hurry this step by putting it in the refrigerator.)

2. Then mix until creamy the margarine, shortening, sugar, and vanilla. Finally, add the cooled flour/milk mixture and beat at high speed until frosting is the consistency of whipped cream.

3. Apply only to a *thoroughly cooled cake* or it will look like glaciers in global warming rather than that beautiful feather boa.

Stu's Cranberry Bread

Here's how Stu makes it. If you follow her directions, you might have hollow-leg teenagers, assorted friends, long-lost relations, street people, and the cable guy falling all over themselves to get a warm, moist slice. Make that two. Okay, three.

1. Preheat oven to 350 degrees. Grease loaf pan.
2. In a mixer, cream together butter and sugar. Beat in egg yolks and orange rind until blended.
3. In a separate bowl, sift together flower, baking powder, baking soda, and salt. Add the flour mixture to the batter alternately with the orange juice. Gently mix in the cranberries.
4. In a separate bowl, beat egg whites until stiff and fold them carefully into the batter, stirring as little as possible. Pour batter into prepared pan and set on middle rack of the oven. Bake for 50-60 minutes. (You can cover with tinfoil if the top is getting too brown before the middle is done.) Meanwhile, prepare the glaze.
5. Combine orange juice and sugar in a small saucepan and simmer for about 5-7 minutes, until a light syrup forms.
6. Prick the hot bread with a thin skewer or toothpick. Spoon the hot syrup over the hot bread as soon as it is removed from the oven. Cool in the pan on a wire rack.

Bread

1 stick butter, softened

¾ cup granulated sugar

2 egg yolks (reserve whites)

Grated rind of 1 or 2 small oranges

1½ cups all-purpose flour

1½ tsp. baking powder

¼ tsp. baking soda

Pinch of salt

½ cup fresh orang juice

1 cup cranberries, chopped

Glaze

¼ cup orange juice

¼ cup sugar

(***NOTE***: For a cake: pour batter into a 10-inch Bundt pan, greased with vegetable shortening *and* pan spray. Bake 30-35 minutes. Cool 5 minutes, remove from Bundt pan, glaze.)

Delores's Pan de Polvo (Mexican Wedding Cookies)

Ahh, sweet! José Enriques showed up on the Baxters' doorstep (to see Amanda, of course) with his mother's yummy Mexican Wedding Cookies in hand. Was there a hidden message in there? But obviously, you don't have to wait for a Mexican wedding to serve these delectable cookies!

2 tsp. anise seeds
3 sticks cinnamon
5 cups flour
1½ tsp. baking powder
1 tsp. salt
1½ cups shortening (lard is more authentic)
3 cups sugar
2 Tbsp. ground cinnamon

1. Boil the anise seeds and cinnamon sticks in about 1 cup of water until it produces a strong tea. Remove seeds and cinnamon sticks and allow to cool. Mix the flour, baking powder and salt, then cut in the shortening until the mixture resembles coarse corn meal. Finally combine 2 cups of the sugar. (Reserve the third cup for the coating.) When it is evenly mixed, begin adding the anise tea until the dough is well blended. You may have to knead the dough by hand.

2. *Either* (1) roll out a little at a time with a floured rolling pin on a floured surface until ¼ inch thick. Use a small cookie cutter and place the cookies on an un-greased cookie sheet. *Or* (2) flour your hands, and roll a handful of dough into a log about 1 inch in diameter and about 12 inches long. Cut log into ¼ inch thick "wheels." Place on an un-greased cookie sheet.

3. Bake in a pre-heated oven at 375 degrees until golden brown (15-20 min.). While baking, mix the remaining cup of sugar and 2 tablespoons of ground cinnamon in a bowl. When the cookies are done, remove and, while still warm, roll in the cinnamon-sugar.

Makes about 4 dozen cookies.

Jodi's Green Beans and Brown Butter Rotini

Bonus (not previously included)

2 Tbs. salt

1 lb. rotini pasta

1 lb. fresh green beans cut into two-inch lengths

4 Tbs. (½ stick) real butter

1 cup chopped walnuts

⅛ tsp. red pepper flakes

½ cup freshly grated Parmesan cheese

Just arrived home from work before your hungry family tumbles through the door? ACK! What can you fix? Jodi Baxter is likely to think pasta! and be praised by Denny as "some kind of a gourmet cook" just before he grabs her and gives her a big hug. Don't know what will happen at your house but give this one a try. It's sure to please!

1. Bring 5 quarts of water to a boil in a large pot. Add 2 Tbs. of salt and the green beans. Cook just until tender, about 5 minutes. With a large slotted spoon or skimmer transfer the beans into a colander to drain, and then place into a bowl.

2. Add the rotini to the boiling water and cook according to package directions, stirring occasionally to prevent the pasta from sticking together.

3. Meanwhile, melt the butter in a large frying pan over low heat. Skim off most of the foaming, white solid and discard. Continue cooking until the butter turns golden brown (about 2 minutes) but be careful that it doesn't burn. Add the walnuts and red pepper flakes, and salt to taste. (Without making the dish noticeably spicy, a few red pepper flakes perk up many pasta dishes.)

4. Set your colander in your serving bowl in the bottom of your sink and empty the pasta into the colander, allowing the hot water to fill your serving dish to warm it while

the pasta drains. After a minute or so, dump out the water, dry the serving dish, and transfer the rotini into it. Add the green beans and the sauce and toss lightly until evenly mixed. Check to see if you need more salt. If the sauce seems too thick, add a few tablespoons of the pasta water.

5. Top with Parmesan cheese and serve with a fruit salad (canned pineapple chunks, canned mandarin orange slices, and seedless red grapes), and toasted garlic bread.

A quick meal for a hungry 4.

Recipes from Book Three

About the book:

The Yada Yadas thought they had a handle on forgiveness, but it seems God has them on a crash-course to an even deeper level.

From Jodi's Journal: "After everything the Yada Yadas have been through in the past eight months, I told God I could sure use a little 'dull and boring' in the new year! But that was before Leslie 'Stu' Stuart moved in upstairs. Ms. Perfect herself and me living in the same two-flat? If I can't manage perfect patience—and do a lot of tongue-biting—it'll be a recipe for collision. Then Delores Enriquez's son Jose wanted to throw my Amanda a *Quinceañera*—a coming-out party, Mexican style—and they're only fifteen!

"At least Bandana Woman, who held up our Yada Yada Prayer Group at knife-point last fall, was safely locked up in prison . . . or so I thought. But then she ends up back in our face. I mean, how far is forgiveness supposed to go?

"I'd been asking God for a little 'dull and boring' this year. Instead, it seems like opening my life to His plans just results in a life of unpredictability—in the best and hardest ways.

"I guess I should have realized that with eleven Yada Yada sisters as diverse as a bag of Jelly Bellies, life would always be unpredictable. All I know is that the longer we pray together, the more 'real' things are getting, not only with each other but with God. Dull and boring? Not a chance."

In the meantime . . .

As usual, the Yada Yada sisters always find time to bring out the food, even when life is unpredictable. You can't really read *The Yada Yada Prayer Group Gets Real* without your mouth watering. But, good news, you can do something about it! Try one or all of the following recipes and add them to your Family Favorites.

Delores's Easy Carnitas

And we thought making the traditional "carnitas" would be hard! Give this recipe a try and we guarantee it'll become a favorite to serve over rice, roll up in a tortilla, or use as the meat in your tacos.

1½ pound boneless pork shoulder, cut into 1-inch cubes (beef may be substituted)

2 Tbsp. brown sugar

1 Tbsp. molasses

2 tsp. powdered beef bouillon or 2 cubes

½ tsp. cayenne

1 tsp. cumin

4 cloves garlic, finely diced

1 can Pepsi or Coke (diet soda is okay)

Garnish

3 scallions (green onions) sliced

Fresh cilantro

Juice of 1-2 limes

Hot sauce to taste

1. Place all the ingredients except the Pepsi in a deep, cast-iron skillet over a high flame.

2. Once the meat begins to sear, add half of the can of Pepsi and allow it to boil nearly away, stirring repeatedly. This will take about 20 minutes.

3. Then add the remaining Pepsi a little at a time as the syrup caramelizes and adheres to the meat. Stir so that nothing sticks and burns. When most of the Pepsi has evaporated (about another 10 minutes), turn off the flame.

4. Serve over a bed of rice, or use as the meat in tacos, or serve with toothpicks as an appetizer.

5. Add garnish. Include other favorite ingredients (lettuce, tomatoes, cheese, onions, etc.) if you are making tacos.

Serves 4 (or about 8 as appetizers).

Jodi's Cheese Soufflé with Mushroom Sauce

Jodi prepares this when she wants to pamper her family or guests. But she's learned from sad experience to put up signs saying, "DO NOT SLAM DOORS" and to shut Willy Wonka in a bedroom, otherwise her soufflé might fall like the lopsided top hat worn by Cat in a Hat. But her family always loves it anyway. So give it a try!

Soufflé

6 Tbsp. (¾ of a stick) butter

6 Tbsp. all-purpose flour

1½ cups milk

¾ tsp. salt

¼ tsp. cayenne

¾ pound sharp cheddar cheese grated or thinly sliced

6 eggs (at room temperature)

½ tsp. cream of tartar

Sauce

6 medium mushrooms, sliced

1 garlic cloves, finely diced

1 can cream of mushroom soup

Thin with ⅓ cup water or white wine

1. Make sure your eggs are at room temperature, so your soufflé will rise better.
2. Melt butter, blend in the flour. Gradually add milk and cook over low heat until thick, stirring constantly. Add salt, cayenne, and the grated cheese. Stir until cheese melts. Remove mixture from heat.
3. Thoroughly separate egg yolks from the whites. To do this, crack the egg over one bowl, letting the egg white slide out of the shell. Then dump the yolk in another bowl. Don't let any yolk mix in the whites.
4. Beat the yolks until thick and smooth. Slowly add the cheese mixture to egg yolks, stirring constantly.
5. Let the mixture cool while you beat the egg whites and cream of tartar (with *clean* beaters) until they stand up stiff but haven't started to dry out or break apart.
6. Slowly pour the cheese/yolk mixture into the whipped egg whites, gently folding it together with a spatula or wooden spoon that doesn't cut through the egg whites. It does not

need to be completely mixed, and excessive stirring or jarring will deflate the egg whites.

7. Carefully pour the mixture into an ungreased 2 qt. soufflé or casserole dish. For a "top hat" effect (it puffs in the oven!), trace a circle through mixture 1 inch from the edge and 1 inch deep.

8. Bake in a thoroughly preheated oven at 350 degrees for 30 minutes or until a knife comes out clean, but do not open the oven door until it has cooked at least 20 minutes.

9. Bring the soufflé gently to the table to be served immediately. (If the weather or Willy Wonka doesn't knock it down, waiting will.)

Sauce: Fifteen minutes before the soufflé is done baking, lightly sauté the sliced mushrooms and garlic in the bottom of a saucepan using a little butter. Add a can of cream of mushroom soup, and ⅓ can liquid (water or white wine) and bring to a low simmer, stirring to avoid sticking. Ladle the mushroom sauce over individual helpings of soufflé like gravy.

Alternative: Don't have time to make the sauce? Open and heat a jar of marinara sauce and ladle it over individual helpings of the soufflé. Or, offer both sauces to your hungry crowd.

Serves 4-6.

Stu's Spaghetti alla Carbonara

Legend has it that this dish was originally popularized by the charcoal makers of ancient Italy because the word carbone is Italian for coal. "But there was nothing 'black' in the restaurant versions I've had," explains Stu, "so I fixed it by adding sliced black olives." Well, that's Stu! But it tastes good, so who's going to complain? Oh. One more thing. Preparing carbonara definitely requires a third hand, someone to help you with the final mixing . . . but somehow Stu manages to do it by herself. Go figure.

1 pound spaghetti

½ pound bacon, cut into bits

6 eggs

6 cloves garlic, finely diced

½ cup half-and-half, or soy milk

½ cup grated Parmesan cheese

4 oz. can of sliced black olives, drained

Freshly ground black pepper

1. While cooking the pasta according to the directions on the package, fry the bacon until just crispy, add the garlic 1 minute before the bacon is done. (Frying garlic until it browns causes it to lose its garlic flavor and become bitter.) While these ingredients cook, blend the eggs, half-and-half, and salt.
2. When you have drained the pasta, put it in a large bowl while still hot. Then, with one hand remove the pan with the still bubbling bacon and garlic, and with the other hand pick up the blender with the eggs mixture. With your "third hand" (see, Stu must have one), stir the pasta vigorously while pouring the hot bacon bits and grease and the egg mixture simultaneously into the hot pasta. The heat from the bacon grease and pasta will cook the eggs.
3. Toss in the grated Parmesan cheese, sliced olives, and sprinkle liberally with freshly ground black pepper. Serve with a tossed green salad, garlic bread, and a rich red wine.

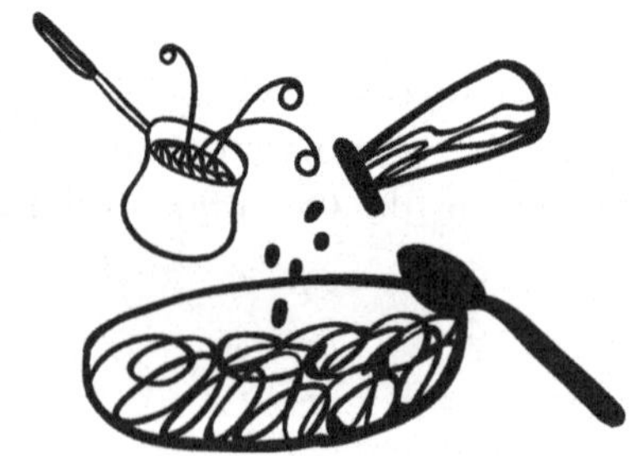

Serves 4-6.

Jodi's Chicken Breasts in Mango Sauce

Once you make this, you'll know why Jodi considers this one of the Baxter five-star meals—good and easy. Your dinner guests will think you're a gourmet cook! But hey, if the chicken breasts are thawed and your ingredients are at hand, you should be able to get dinner on the table in less than 30 minutes with no problem. We won't tell.

6 skinless, boneless chicken breasts

¼ tsp. salt

¼ tsp. pepper

2 Tbsp. butter

1 peeled and diced mango

1 cup orange juice

½ cup apricot jam

1½ Tbsp. spicy mustard

Fresh parsley (optional)

1. Salt and pepper the chicken breasts and sauté them in butter in a nonstick skillet until golden brown on both sides.

2. While the chicken is cooking mix the mango, orange juice, apricot jam, and mustard in a bowl until the jam dissolves into the juice.

3. Add the mango mixture to the chicken and bring to a boil. Reduce the heat and simmer for about 12 minutes, turning the chicken occasionally.

4. When the chicken is done and the sauce has thickened, lift out the chicken breasts and arrange on a serving platter. Pour the mangos and sauce over the chicken and garnish with sprigs of fresh parsley.

Serve with white rice and a green vegetable.

Note: Don't know how to cut a mango? See instructions on page 84.

Serves 4-6.

Jodi's Lemony Bundt Cake

The hardest part of this recipe is getting the cake out of the Bundt pan in one piece! But it's one of the Baxter all-time favorites, so if at first you don't succeed, try, try again. It's worth it!

Cake:

1 package lemon cake mix

1 regular-size package lemon instant pudding (Or use 1 regular-size package lemon Jello dissolved in 1 cup boiling water)

4 eggs

½ cup vegetable oil

1 cup water (if using instant pudding)

Topping:

1⅓ cup confectioners' sugar

5 Tbsp. fresh lemon juice

Plus . . . Vegetable shortening and non-stick pan spray

1. Heat oven to 350 degrees. Evenly grease *and* spray a heavy Bundt cake pan with a nonstick spray; dust it with flour. All three steps are crucial in getting it to fall free from the Bundt pan in one piece.
2. Place cake mix, instant pudding, eggs, vegetable oil, and water in a large mixing bowl. (If using lemon Jello, dissolve it in 1 cup *boiling* water before adding to the mixing bowl.) Beat with a mixer on medium speed for 2 to 3 minutes, scraping down the edges of the bowl occasionally with a spatula.
3. Pour into the prepared Bundt pan and bake for 35 minutes. Cool cake pan on a wire cake rack for about 5 minutes before putting your cake plate over the top, turning it upside down, and gently tapping the pan until the cake drops onto the plate, hopefully in one piece.
4. Perforate the cake with a small skewer or toothpick so the frosting can soak in. Blend together the confectioners' sugar and lemon juice, and slowly spoon it over the top and sides of the warm cake, covering as much of the cake as possible. The cake is best when chilled.
5. For a finishing touch, use a wire mesh strainer to dust confectioner's sugar over the rounded top of the cake.

Serves 8-10.

Delores's Homemade Salsa

Bonus (not previously included)

- **1 large can (28 oz.) petite diced tomatoes**
- **1 small onion, diced**
- **1 small serrano chili pepper, finely chopped**
- **juice of 1 large or 2 small limes**
- **1 cup chopped cilantro**
- **1 Tbsp. sugar**
- **1 tsp. salt**
- **1 Tbsp. cornstarch**

Homemade salsa with fresh tomatoes and a little zing (mm-mmm!) tends to make one want to . . . dance the Salsa! (Store-bought salsa is just never as good as homemade.) But in the winter it's nearly impossible to get tomatoes that taste like home-grown. And they're the best.

But (shhhh) Delores has agreed to share her little trick: Start with a can of petite diced tomatoes and add the other ingredients fresh. See, canning companies don't have to pick tomatoes two weeks in advance to get them to market before they spoil. They can leave them on the vine until they're perfectly ripe and then process them within hours. So, here goes . . .

1. Drain the tomatoes into a colander, reserving ½ cup of the juice. While you chop the other ingredients, allow the tomatoes to drain several minutes, turning them over in the colander a couple times without crushing them.
2. In a sauce pan, stir and dissolve the cornstarch into the reserved tomato juice and heat it until it just begins to bubble, stirring regularly. Remove it from the heat and put it in the freezer. Once it is cool, combine this thickening in a bowl with all the other ingredients and stir only until mixed evenly.
3. Chill and serve with chips or on tacos, tostados, or quesadillas.

Serves 6.

(***Note:*** One serrano chili pepper will produce a medium-hot salsa. Use more or less to taste. Be sure to chop it very finely, but be careful! Even after you wash your hands, it will still feel like fire if you rub your eyes. You might want to use rubber or latex gloves.)

Yo-Yo's Lentils with Honey and Bacon

Bonus (not previously included)

- 2 ⅓ cups (1 lb.) dry lentils
- 1 bay leaf
- 2 tsp. salt
- ¼ lb. bacon (4 to 6 slices)
- 1 Tbsp. Dijon mustard or 1 tsp. dry mustard
- 1 Tbsp. fresh ginger, grated (or ¼ tsp. powdered ginger)
- 1 Tbsp. soy sauce
- 1 medium onion, chopped
- ½ cup honey

Yo-Yo may be blunt and honest. But she's also raising her two teenage brothers who EAT! So, when she can't get them to make their own peanut butter sandwiches, she goes for anything cheap, quick, filling, and GOOD! And one of her favorites is "Lentils with Honey and Bacon." You can replace the bacon with sausage or ground beef, but her brothers won't do the total vegan thing (though this is a good one to try if you substitute the meat with a couple tablespoons of olive oil).

So, hike up those bib overalls, and give it a try!

1. In a medium sauce pan, combine the lentils, bay leaf, and salt in 5 cups of water and bring to a boil. Reduce heat, cover, and simmer for 30 minutes.

2. In the meantime, cut the bacon into bits and fry until it just begins to crisp. Remove and drain.

3. Mix the remaining ingredients (mustard, ginger, soy sauce, onion, and honey) with 1 cup of water.

4. When the lentils have simmered for 30 minutes, remove the bay leaf and stir all ingredients together in a 3 to 4-quart casserole dish, reserving a few bacon bits to sprinkle on top.

5. Cover and bake in a 350-degree oven for one hour.

Serve over rice. Top with a scoop of cottage cheese and sprinkle with hot sauce if desired.

If you're at Yo-Yo's house you might hear: "Hey, get in here and get it or forget it! Ya hear me?"

Serves 4-6.

Recipes from Book Four

About the book:

The Yada Yadas got tight in the past year, but they're about to learn the real meaning of togetherness.

From Jodi's Journal: "We'd done it: we'd taken a mismatched, diverse group of women and cobbled together a prayer group that really worked for all of us. Now that spring was here, we were celebrating our one-year anniversary. We'd had a wild year full of joy, sorrow, and a healthy dose of laughter—lots of laughter—plus wedding, an early parole, and two baptisms in the lake! Everything was feeling pretty great.

"But it's when we're in our comfort zone that we're most likely to let our guard down. Without warning, lots of little things seemed to become big problems. And some don't seem so little, like the white supremacy hate group targeting a local university and viciously attacking Nony's husband, whose very life is hanging in the balance. Suddenly, the very diversity of our group feels like a liability. But that vicious attack on Nony's husband made us see we had to get tough—and fight back together."

About the recipes:

The season of the year featured in *The Yada Yada Prayer Group Gets Tough* is May and June, which doesn't have a lot of holiday celebrations with traditional foods. (Well, there's Pentecost Sunday and Memorial Day; also Mother's Day and Father's Day. Maybe you have favorite recipes for these celebrations!)

But between holidays, you still have to eat, right? So here are some of Jodi Baxter's Five-Star Recipes—and to rate Five Stars at the Baxter household, the food has to be easy to make *and* really tasty.

Seven-Layer Make-Ahead Salad

Or Six-Layer or Eight-Layer—it kind of depends what you have on hand! Have at it, be sure to let it chill to marinate, and serve it at your next gathering of hungry folks. You probably won't have any leftovers, which will disappoint the dog unless you let it lick the dish clean. (What? Your dog doesn't like salad? Willie Wonka does. Of course, Willie Wonka will eat anything in a people dish.)

1 head iceberg lettuce, chopped or torn into bite-size pieces

1 cup diced celery

6 hardboiled eggs, sliced

1 ten-ounce package frozen peas (do not thaw)

½ red onion, finely diced

8 slices bacon, crispy-fried and crumbled into bits

2 cups mayonnaise with 2 Tbsp. sugar mixed in

1 cup grated cheddar cheese

1. Layer vegetables, eggs, and bacon in the order listed into a large, flat dish such as a 9" x 13" cake pan,.
2. Salt and pepper to taste. You can also sprinkle each layer with a little sugar.
3. Spread the dressing over the salad and sprinkle with cheese.
4. If desired, garnish with sliced green onions and paprika. Cover and refrigerate 8-12 hours. Then go put your feet up and whisk it out of the refrigerator when it comes time to head out the door to the next church potluck or Yada Yada meeting.

Serves 4-6.

Jodi's Secret Spaghetti Sauce

Denny swears this is the best spaghetti sauce he's ever eaten. Okay, he could be a bit prejudiced. Or loyal. (Or just plain savvy!) But the recipe was tested and re-tested, and we think he may be right!

1 lb. lean ground beef

2 medium (or 1 large) onions, chopped

½ lb. mushrooms, sliced

1 28-ounce can tomatoes

1 6-ounce can tomato paste plus 1 can water

2-3 tsp. basil

2-3 tsp. oregano

1-2 tsp. salt (to taste)

1 Tbsp. sugar or honey

4 garlic cloves, crushed or finely diced

1. Brown the ground beef in the bottom of the pot you will be using to make the sauce.
2. Turn down the heat and add the onions and mushrooms.
3. While they are cooking, blend the tomatoes, tomato paste, and water.
4. When onions and mushrooms are soft, pour off any extra grease from the meat, and add the blended tomatoes and remaining spices. Simmer 15-20 minutes.
5. Meanwhile, cook 1 lb. spaghetti or pasta according to package directions, drain, load each plate with pasta, and pass the sauce and grated Parmesan cheese. (Tossed green salad and hot garlic bread are *de rigor*, of course.)

Serves 4-6.

Hamburger Vegetable Soup

Really. Try it. This is a truly satisfying soup, robust enough for a main dish, and if you make a LOT, you've got a few extra lunches and midnight snacks covered. And oh, yes, it's healthy, too, with all those veggies.

1 6-ounce can tomato paste

2 finely diced garlic cloves

2 medium (or 1 large) onions, chopped

4 stalks celery, chopped

4 unpeeled carrots, sliced thin

4 medium potatoes, diced

4 Tbsp. beef bouillon (powdered) or 4 cubes

1 crushed bay leaf

1 pinch of marjoram, thyme, or savory (or all three)

½ tsp. freshly ground peppercorns

2 ½ qts. vegetable cooking water (plain water can be substituted)

1 lb. lean ground beef

1. Combine all the ingredients (except the ground beef) in a large kettle and bring to a boil. Simmer, covered, until the vegetables are almost tender (about 10-15 minutes).

2. Add the ground beef by crumbling it into small pieces and stir just until it loses its pinkness. Bring the soup again to a simmer and serve.

Serves 6-8 when served with cornbread, butter, and honey.

Dressy Bow-Tie Pasta Salad

Whoa! Based on requests for this recipe, Jodi Baxter may have to up her scale to Ten Stars. Be sure to double this recipe for a crowd, adjust the ingredients to "more or less," and just be sure to leave enough time for all that chopping and slicing. Can be made ahead of time and chilled—just add the dressing at the last minute so the spinach doesn't wilt.

8 oz. bow-tie pasta

¼ cup fresh lemon juice

1 Tbsp. lemon zest (grated lemon peel)

4 cloves garlic, finely minced

⅓ cup extra virgin olive oil

2 large boneless chicken breasts, cooked and cubed (or 3 cups cooked chicken)

2-3 cups chopped spinach

1½ cups cucumber (peel, halve lengthwise, and then slice)

1½ cups red seedless grapes, halved

2 celery sticks, thinly sliced

½ cup sliced green onions

½ cup chopped pecans

1. While cooking the pasta according to the instructions on the package, blend thoroughly (in a blender or with a wire whisk) the lemon juice, zest, garlic, and olive oil to make dressing.

2. When the pasta is done, drain and rinse with cold water to cool.

3. Then in a large pasta bowl combine the pasta, chicken, spinach, cucumber, grapes, celery, and onions.

4. Pour the dressing over the salad and toss gently. Sprinkle with pecans.

Serves 6. Consider serving with toasted garlic bread, corn on the cob, and iced tea on a hot summer day.

Nony's Sugary Lemon Bars

Bonus (not previously included)

You've been asked to bring dessert to a party . . . uh oh. Don't they know your dessert repertoire consists of a half-gallon of ice cream or store-bought cookies? Take a tip from Jodi Baxter (who's also dessert-challenged) who begged Nonyameko Sisulu-Smith for her recipe for Sugary Lemon Bars, and you'll have people begging YOU for the recipe!

2 cups all-purpose flour

1 cup (2 sticks) butter or margarine, softened

1 cup confectioners' (powdered) sugar

4 eggs, beaten

1 cup sugar

1 tsp. baking powder

1 tsp. salt

¼ cup fresh lemon juice

1 Tbs. finely grated lemon peel

1. Preheat oven to 350 degrees.
2. Using a pastry blender, thoroughly mix the flour, butter, and confectioners' sugar.
3. Press mixture evenly into the bottom of a 9 x 13-inch baking pan.
4. Bake for 20 minutes or until lightly browned. While it is baking, mix together the remaining ingredients. Remove from oven and pour the mixture over the "crust."
5. Return to the oven and continue baking for another 20 minutes.
6. Remove from the oven and loosen from the edge of the pan with a knife and allow to cool. After cooling, cut into bars and dust with more confectioners' sugar.

Yields approximately 24-30 sweet & tart bars.

Recipes from Book Five

About the book:

For the Yada prayer sisters and their families, getting caught up in troubles isn't the problem; it's how to get free.

From Jodi's Journal: "Only weeks ago, we Yada Yada sisters toughened our prayer knees when one of our own was the victim of a vicious, racial attack. Now it seems each household is being thrown into even bigger and badder circumstances. It especially worries me. I'm a fixer by nature, and our prayer list is getting out of control . . .

"Ruth and Ben are caught in an unplanned pregnancy—in their fifties! Chanda is deluded by the glitter of her lottery dream come true. Florida wants to move her family, hoping to leave trouble behind, but it looks like it may catch up to her anyway. Avis is torn between honoring her new husband and helping her abused adult daughter, who keeps running home to Mama. And I'm finding that even good things like the prayer group can consume us in no time flat.

"Maybe our best hope is to catch on to what God's doing—and catch on quick!—before the enemy can take any prisoners. That'd be a freedom worth celebrating. And celebrating is what I and my spiritual sisters do best!"

And celebrations usually mean food!

One of the best things about getting together with a group of sisters to eat and celebrate, is that the food on the table is often a collection of tried-and-true family recipes. Which is what the Yada Yada sisters are sharing here, so you better appreciate it! Adele wasn't so sure she wanted to give up her family recipe for Southern Fried Chicken, but Nony quoted her a Scripture verse about things hidden in secret will come to the light anyway, so give it a try from page 114.

Becky's First-Ever Chocolate Cake

This is really Jodi's recipe, but Becky was so excited to discover how easy it is, she made it every time she was supposed to bring something to Yada Yada or a church potluck, and pretty soon everyone thought of it as "Becky's Chocolate Cake." It's dark, moist, and chocolate-ty. But Becky usually doubles the recipe.

Cake

1½ cups flour
3 Tbsp. cocoa
1 tsp. soda
1 cup sugar
½ tsp. salt
5 Tbsp. vegetable oil
1 Tbsp. vinegar
1 tsp. vanilla
1 cup cold water

1. Sift directly into a greased 9 x 9-inch cake pan (or 9 x 13 if you double the recipe) the flour, cocoa, soda, sugar, and salt.
2. Make three "wells" into this dry mixture, pouring oil into one, vinegar into another, and the vanilla into the third.
3. Pour the cup of cold water over it all and stir everything together just like you did in the sandbox when you were four years old. Continue stirring until it is smooth and the flour is no longer visible.
4. Bake at 350 degrees for 30 minutes. Then frost with your favorite chocolate frosting. If you don't have one, here's . . .

Easy-Does-It Chocolate Frosting

Frosting

1 cup sugar
¼ cup cocoa
¼ cup butter
¼ cup milk
1 tsp. vanilla

1. In a saucepan over medium heat, mix everything together except the vanilla. Bring to a boil for 1 minute.
2. Remove from the heat and add the vanilla.
3. Cool partially and transfer to a small Pyrex or metal mixing bowl and beat with an electric mixer until spreadable (about 3 minutes). Frosts one 9 x 9-inch cake.

Adele's Southern Fried Chicken

Adele always starts the night before so the chicken can marinate in the buttermilk to adequately tenderize and flavor it. When Jodi tried this recipe, she had to stick a big note on the kitchen cupboard and set an alarm to remind her. (Starting stuff the night before isn't usually on her list of requirements for Five-Star Baxter Favorites.) But now she says, "Hey, using already cut up chicken pieces and pouring buttermilk over them took all of about five minutes. If I can do it, you can too."

3½ to 4-lb. chicken, cut into pieces

2 cups buttermilk

1 tsp. black pepper

¼ tsp. salt

1¼ cups all-purpose flour

1½ tsp. seasoned salt (or ½ tsp. each of garlic powder, salt, and paprika)

2 cups vegetable oil (or 1 lb. lard if you want to be truly authentic)

1 stick butter

1. Rinse the chicken pieces and blot them with paper towels.

2. In a large bowl combine the buttermilk, ¼ teaspoon of the black pepper and the salt, and stir to combine. Add the chicken pieces and turn to coat evenly.

3. Cover and refrigerate several hours (overnight if possible), turning the pieces occasionally to keep them well coated.

4. Combine the flour, seasoned salt, and the remaining ¾ teaspoon of black pepper in a double paper bag. (Two bags, so they won't tear.)

5. Put the vegetable oil and butter in a large cast-iron frying pan or pot big enough to hold the chicken pieces in one layer without touching. Melt over medium-high heat. The oil should be about ½-inch deep. Heat to 365 degrees on an instant-read thermometer or a candy thermometer.

6. Remove the thighs from the buttermilk marinade, and drop them into the bag of flour mixture. Close the top, and give a couple shakes until chicken pieces are coated.

7. Place the thighs skin-side down in the center of the pan. (Thighs will require the longest time to cook.)

8. Coat the remaining pieces in the same way and add them to the pan in a single layer without touching. Work in batches if necessary.

9. Don't move the chicken until the coating sets (about 5 minutes). Lift and check the underside until it is deep golden, then turn.

10. Cook the pieces between 8 and 20 minutes (depending on size) until crispy, golden, and cooked through. Test doneness by cutting into the thickest part of a meat or inserting an instant-read thermometer. The juices should run clear with no sign of blood. Place on a paper-lined baking sheet to drain.

Serves 4-6. (Of course, Adele always serves Southern Fried Chicken with her Foot-Stompin' Greens. You can find that recipe on page 81.)

Mom Jennings' Christmas Cinnamon Rolls

Okay, so it's not Christmas. Jodi's mom made them for Christmas morning in Book 7, The Yada Yada Prayer Group Gets Decked Out . . . whoops, getting ahead of ourselves. But this is the recipe Jodi used when she made cinnamon rolls for the work crew at the new church—and who said you had to wait till Christmas for cinnamon rolls, anyway?

Dough:

1 cup milk

½ cup (1 stick) butter or margarine

½ cup sugar

1 tsp. salt

2 packets dry yeast

2 eggs, beaten

4½ cups flour

Filling:

½ cup (1 stick) butter or margarine (at room temperature or melted)

¾ cup brown sugar

1 Tbsp. cinnamon

½ cup raisins

½ cup chopped walnuts or pecans (optional)

Dough:

1. Scald the milk; pour into the large bowl of your mixer. Stir in the butter, sugar, and salt.

2. Cool to lukewarm; stir in the yeast. Add eggs and mix.

3. Add about half of the flour and beat with the mixer until smooth.

4. Then add the rest by mixing and kneading with the dough hooks (or by hand) until the dough is smooth and elastic.

5. Cover with a damp cloth or plastic wrap and let rise in a warm place (about 82 degrees) until double in volume. It usually takes an hour or two.

6. Punch it down, cover it again, and let it rest while you soften the filling butter slightly in a microwave (if necessary) and chop the nuts for the filling.

Making the cinnamon rolls:

1. Roll out the dough on a floured board into a rectangle shape to a thickness of ⅜" to ½".

2. Spread evenly with softened butter. Sprinkle with brown sugar, cinnamon, raisins, and/or nuts.

3. Starting from the long edge, roll up the dough into a "log" with the filling spiraled inside.

4. Cut 12 "wheels" 1-inch to 1½-inch thick from the "log" and arrange them loosely (a spiral side up) in a greased 9 x 13-inch baking dish.

5. Cover and allow to rise again for one hour. Brush with egg white, then bake at 350 degrees for 40 minutes or until light golden brown.

Optional: Glaze with 1 cup confectioners' sugar, adding just enough water (start with 1 Tbsp.) to get your desired thinness. Dribble over the cooled cinnamon rolls in swirls.

Serves 6. Maybe.

Denny's Summer Mint Salad

Bonus (not previously included)

Few salads have as light and fresh a taste as this one Denny Baxter tosses, and it goes so great with Jodi's lasagna. But because it's one of his few culinary successes, we had to bribe him to reveal its secrets.

1 head romaine lettuce

1 cup shredded red cabbage

1 (loosely packed) cup chopped, fresh mint leaves

2 cups toasted bread croutons

Dressing:

6 drops mint extract

½ tsp. salt

¼ tsp. black pepper

1 tsp. sugar

⅓ cup red wine vinegar

3 Tbs. extra virgin olive oil

1. Be sure the head of romaine lettuce is as crisp and fresh as possible. One trick in shopping is to examine the cut stem end of the head. In general, the less rusty-red on the cut, the fresher the head, but also be sure the leaves aren't starting to wilt.

2. Remove the ends of any wilting leaves, and cut the head crosswise in 3/4-inch strips, discarding the solid core near the stem. Gently break apart the strips, wash in cold water, and spin dry.

3. Dump the lettuce into your favorite salad bowl (clear glass if possible so the salad can be seen), add the shredded red cabbage, mint leaves, and croutons. Toss lightly to distribute evenly.

4. Mix all the ingredients for the dressing, taking care to dissolve the sugar and salt, which may require extra stirring.

5. Wait until people are actually ready to eat before drizzling the dressing over the salad and tossing it one last time. The trick to its fresh taste is immediate consumption.

Jodi's Classic Lasagna

When in doubt what to serve the hungry masses, make lasagna! Jodi uses the same "Secret Spaghetti Sauce" recipe she developed over the years (see page 108), but she makes it a bit thicker here so the lasagna isn't "sloppy."

Sauce:

1 lb. lean ground beef

2 medium (or 1 large) onions, chopped*

½ lb. mushrooms, sliced

1 28-ounce can tomatoes (whole, diced, or crushed)

2 6-ounce cans tomato paste plus 1 can water

2 tsp. basil

2 tsp. oregano

1-2 tsp. salt (to taste)

4 garlic cloves, crushed or finely diced

And you'll need . . .

½ lb. lasagna noodles (9 noodles) cooked till *al dente*

1 pint cottage cheese

½ lb. (8 oz.) mozzarella cheese, grated

½ cup parmesan cheese, grated

1. Brown the ground beef in the bottom of the pot in which you will be making the sauce. Add the onions and mushrooms.

2. Blend the tomatoes, tomato paste, and water in your blender. When the beef is cooked, pour off any extra grease and add the blended tomatoes and spices. Simmer 15-20 minutes.

3. While the sauce is simmering, cook the lasagna noodles according to package directions, then drain and rinse in cool water.

4. Spread a small amount of the sauce over the bottom of a 9 x 13-inch baking dish. Then arrange three noodles lengthwise, cover with ⅓ of the tomato sauce, ½ of the cottage cheese, and ⅓ of the mozzarella cheese. Repeat for a second layer. Top that with the final three lasagna noodles, the remaining sauce, the remaining mozzarella cheese, and the parmesan cheese.

5. Bake for 30 minutes at 350 degrees. Remove and cool for 10 minutes before serving with a tossed green salad and hot garlic bread.

Serves 4-6 very happy campers.

Lemon and Thyme Chicken Breasts

This one is high on the list of Five-Star Baxter favorites. First, because it's simple (yea for sales on boneless chicken breasts!). Second, because it's delicious. If you like lemon, this one is guaranteed to be a family favorite.

3 Tbsp. flour

½ tsp. salt

¼ tsp. pepper

4 boneless, skinless chicken breasts halves

2 Tbsp. olive oil

1 medium onion, chopped

1 Tbsp. butter1 cup chicken broth (or 1 cup water and 1 tsp. chicken bouillon)

3 Tbsp. lemon juice (fresh if possible)

1 Tbsp. fresh or ½ Tbsp. dry thyme

Lemon wedges

2 Tbsp. chopped, fresh parsley

1. Shake the flour, salt, and pepper together in a lunch-size paper bag. Add the chicken and shake to coat. (Save the excess seasoned flour.)
2. Put the chicken breasts into a large skillet in which you have heated a tablespoon of olive oil over a medium heat. Brown the chicken on one side (about 5 minutes) and turn. Add the second tablespoon of olive oil, and brown on the second side.
3. Remove and set the chicken aside. Melt the butter in the skillet and sauté the onions until translucent. Add the remaining seasoned flour and stir until smooth. Add the chicken broth, thyme, and 2 tablespoons of lemon juice. Stir constantly while you bring the sauce to a boil.
4. Return the chicken to the skillet and reduce the heat to a low simmer. Cover the skillet and cook until the chicken is tender (about 15 minutes).
5. Remove the cooked chicken breasts to your serving plate. Stir the remaining lemon juice into the sauce and pour over the chicken. Garnish with parsley and extra lemon wedges.

Serves 4.

Flo's Mustard Potato Salad

Bonus (not previously included)

Florida says, "What's with all this fancy-dancy salad stuff? When ya gonna throw some chicken on the grill, boil some corn on the cob, and give me a good ol' mustardy potato salad to go with it!"

9 cups peeled and cubed red potatoes (about 3 pounds)
1 large sweet onion, diced
½ cup finely diced celery
½ cup sweet pickle relish or 3 sweet pickles finely diced
4 hard-boiled eggs, coarsely chopped
1 cup mayonnaise
¼ cup chopped fresh parsley
1 tsp. salt
¼ tsp. black pepper
1 tsp. sugar
1 Tbs. cider vinegar
3 Tbs. prepared mustard
Paprika

1. Place peeled and cubed potatoes in kettle, cover with water, and bring to a boil. Cook for 8 minutes or until tender but not mushy.

2. Drain, cover with cold water for 8-10 minutes. Drain again, thoroughly, and place in a large bowl.

3. Add onion, celery, pickles, and eggs. Toss gently.

4. Separately, combine the mayonnaise, parsley, salt, pepper, sugar, vinegar, and mustard. Mix thoroughly and pour over the potatoes.

5. Stir carefully so as not to mash the potatoes. Sprinkle with paprika, cover and refrigerate until chilled.

Serves 10.

Recipes from Book Six

About the book:

A devastating fire wakes up the Yadas to a new reality: God is on the move.

As the Yada Yada Prayer Group hurtles toward the second anniversary of the day they met, little do they know it will be a year of losses and new beginnings. MaDear's failing health stirs the need for deeper healing between Adele and Denny. The props Amanda has been leaning on—Willie Wonka, her lifelong pet, and José Enriques, her teenage love—get knocked out from under her. A major fire at a women's shelter nearly destroys the idealistic intentions of its young volunteers. And Avis faces yet another crushing blow concerning her precious daughter, who just got untangled from an abusive marriage.

From Jodi's Journal: "What I'd like to know is—why does God keep re-arranging my comfort zone? Could it have something to do with my Yada Yada prayer sisters, who aren't afraid to get in each other's faces and tend to expect big things from God?

"But to move forward, sometimes we have to let go of what's behind. In spite of the loss of two dear friends . . . the breakup of a teenage love . . . the curse of HIV . . . prison time hanging over the head of a beloved child. And . . . in spite of fire consuming the hopes of those who have nothing to begin with."

Yet, as the Yada Yada sisters soon discover, God is doing a new thing as they press on, pray on, and get rolling! And of course, God is also full of delightful surprises—like the diamond ring that shows up at the Yada Yada second anniversary fiesta . . .

Warning . . .

Not sure you can make it through *The Yada Yada Prayer Group Gets Rolling* without drooling on the pages. Every time you turn a page, the Yada Yadas are feasting. Again. It was a hard call, which recipes to include in this batch, but here they are.

Quick, into the kitchen, so you can do something besides drool!

Jodi's Lasagna Spinach Roll-Ups

Got vegetarian friends? Or ready for something a bit lighter? Spinach roll-ups are devoured even by carnivores (and even by kids who think they don't like spinach).

1. **Noodles:** Cook the lasagna noodles according to the instructions on the package to the *al dente* stage.

2. **Filling:** Meanwhile, chop and steam the fresh spinach until limp or, if frozen, thaw it in a microwave. Press out excess water from the spinach. Place the spinach in a bowl and add the parmesan cheese, cottage cheese, and nutmeg. Mix this filling well.

3. **Sauce:** Blend the tomatoes, tomato paste, and spices in a blender into a smooth sauce. *Note:* This sauce does not have to be cooked ahead of time.

4. **Assemble:** Lay out the individual noodles side by side on your clean counter and spread a heaping tablespoon of filling along the length of each noodle. Adjust until all the noodles are covered evenly. Roll each one up and lay it on its side in a greased 9 x 13-inch baking pan. Arrange evenly and sprinkle the chopped onions and mozzarella cheese over the roll ups. Cover with the tomato sauce and bake at 350 degrees for about an hour.

Serves 6 when accompanied with a green salad and hot garlic bread.

16 lasagna noodles (a 1-pound package)

2 "bunches" of fresh spinach, chopped, or 2 small boxes of frozen chopped spinach, thawed, drained, and excess water pressed out

¼ to ½ cup grated parmesan cheese

1 pint small curd cottage cheese

½ tsp. nutmeg

1 (28-oz.) can tomatoes

1 6-oz. can tomato paste

4 cloves garlic, minced or crushed

2 tsp. basil

2 tsp. oregano

1 tsp. marjoram

1 medium onion, chopped

2 cups grated mozzarella cheese

Chanda's Easter Buns and Cheese (or Hot Cross Buns)

Chanda and Jodi compared notes and realized that Chanda's Jamaican "Easter Buns" and Jodi's mom's "Hot Cross Buns" were almost identical—except for the cheese.

2 pkgs. dry yeast
⅓ cup milk
1 stick butter
⅓ cup sugar
¾ tsp salt
4 eggs
4 cups flour
⅔ cup raisins or currants
1 Tbsp. cinnamon

Frosting

1½ cups powdered sugar
1½ tsp. finely chopped lemon zest
½ tsp. lemon extract
2 Tbsp. milk
Cheddar cheese for the Jamaican touch

1. Dissolve the yeast in ⅓ cup of warm water and set aside for 10 minutes until the yeast foams to prove it is active.

2. Scald the milk and then combine with butter, sugar, and salt in a large mixing bowl.

3. Stir in 3 beaten eggs (the fourth egg is for egg white to brush on top of the buns), 1 cup of the flour, the activated yeast, and raisins or currants.

4. When smooth, add the remaining 3 cups of flour and the cinnamon.

5. With dough hooks on your mixer or by hand knead until smooth and elastic. (Add a little extra flour if the dough is too sticky to handle.)

6. Cover and set in a warm place to rise for about 2 hours until it doubles in size.

7. Punch down the dough and divide in half repeatedly until you have 16 pieces to form into buns.

8. Flour your hands and roll each bun into a ball. Arrange them on a greased cookie sheet with space to rise.

9. Cover with a towel and allow to rise 1 hour. Just before baking, brush with egg white mixed with a teaspoon of water until frothy.

10. Bake for 12 minutes or until light golden brown in a 375-degree oven.

11. Blend the powdered sugar, lemon zest, lemon extract, and milk. When the buns are cool, drizzle the glaze into the cross on top of each bun.

And for a real Jamaican touch, serve with cheddar cheese.

Makes 16 buns, so you might want to make a double batch, and give some away to your neighbors.

Jodi's "Tunnel of Fudge" Chocolate Cake

Denny has been known to get down on his knees and beg for this cake. It probably won a prize somewhere, but variations of this recipe pop up everywhere. Here's Jodi's version. But beware. You can't make just one and forget it. If you love chocolate, it will haunt you in your sleep.

3½ sticks butter, softened

1 cup granulated sugar

½ cup brown sugar

2 oz. unsweetened chocolate, melted and cooled

6 eggs

2 cups powdered sugar

2¼ cups flour

½ cup cocoa

2 cups walnuts or pecans, chopped

1. Cream the butter, granulated sugar, and brown sugar in a large mixing bowl at high speed until light and fluffy.
2. Add melted and cooled chocolate, beating until combined.
3. Add eggs, one at a time, beating well after each. Gradually add the powdered sugar, continue creaming at high speed.
4. Stop the mixer and by hand, stir in flour, cocoa, and nuts.
5. Pour batter into a well-greased Bundt pan.
6. Bake at 350 degrees for 45-55 minutes or until the top begins to show a shiny, brownie-type crust.
7. Cool for 2 hours before attempting to remove from the pan. Dust the inverted cake with powdered sugar and allow to cool *completely*.

During cooking, some fudge will migrate to the center to create a yummy, gooey tunnel, so testing doneness with a toothpick is ineffective. If you bake it for the shorter time, it will have true fudge in the center. (***Note***: nuts are essential to the success of this recipe.)

Serves 8-10 lucky people.

Jodi's Calico Beans

Forget plain ol' baked beans. These beans are pretty (all those colors!) and tasty, a bit of sweet-and-tangy sauce, and makes enough for a crowd. Just be prepared for everyone to ask you for the recipe.

½ lb. bacon

1 (15-oz.) can green lima beans

1 (15-oz.) can large lima beans (or butter beans)

1 (15-oz.) can black beans

1 (15-oz.) can red beans

1 (15-oz.) can great northern beans

1 (28-oz.) can of pork and beans

2 medium onions chopped

¾ cup brown sugar

2 tsp. salt

1 tsp. dry mustard

3 cloves garlic, minced

½ cup vinegar

½ cup ketchup

1. Cut the bacon into about 1-inch pieces and fry.
2. Meanwhile, drain the cans of beans, reserving the liquid, and put them in a large casserole dish.
3. Just as the bacon begins to crisp, add the onions and fry together.
4. Then add all the other ingredients to the fry pan (except the beans and reserved liquid) and bring to a simmer for 5 minutes.
5. Pour this over the beans and mix thoroughly.
6. Add enough reserved bean liquid to barely cover the beans and bake at 325 degrees for 1½ hours, checking periodically and adding more liquid as needed to keep the beans from drying out.

Serves a crowd. Makes many people happy at your picnic or potluck.

Estelle's Peach Cobbler

Estelle says her mother used to make this with fresh peaches, but canned peaches will do nicely, and it's yummy either way.

1 stick butter

1 cup flour

1½ tsp. baking powder

1¼ cups sugar

¾ cup milk

1 tsp. vanilla

1 (28-oz.) can sliced peaches, drained, juice reserved

1 tsp. cinnamon

¼ cup chopped pecans (optional)

1. Melt butter in a 2-quart casserole dish in a 375-degree oven.
2. While the butter is melting, combine flour, baking powder, and 1 cup of sugar (reserve the rest for the top).
3. Add milk and vanilla to the dry ingredients and stir until blended.
4. Pour the batter into the melted butter. Dribble peach juice into the mixture and arrange the peaches evenly over the batter
5. Scatter pecans on the top and sprinkle with cinnamon and sugar.
6. Bake 30 to 40 minutes until golden brown at 375 degrees.

Serves 4-6 and can be made utterly decadent with scoops of vanilla ice cream.

Jodi's Three-Bean Salad

Bonus (not previously included)

- 1 can cut green beans
- 1 can wax beans
- 1 can kidney beans
- 1 medium onion, chopped
- ¾ cup sugar
- ⅔ cup cider vinegar
- ⅓ cup corn oil
- 1 tsp. salt
- 1 tsp. pepper

Every restaurant salad bar has a three-bean salad, as do most potlucks. "And I usually give them a try," says Denny Baxter. "But if it's not yours, Jodi, I've just wasted the space on my plate."

So, give Jodi's version a try and see if your serving bowl isn't empty by the end of your next picnic or church potluck.

(Double the ingredients if you are taking it to a potluck or picnic.)

1. Drain the beans, then combine all the ingredients, stirring enough to distribute ingredients evenly. Chill overnight.

2. Toss again before serving with a slotted spoon.

Serves 10 . . . unless Denny Baxter shows up.

Ruth's Matzo Ball Soup

You don't have to be Jewish to enjoy Matzo Ball Soup! (Not to mention that matzo balls floating in a yummy chicken broth is probably the most edible way to enjoy matzo!)

Soup:

1 chicken

1 large onion

3 carrots, cut in 1½" segments

4 stalks celery, cut in 1½" segments

2 Tbsp. (or two cubes) chicken bouillon

¼ tsp. pepper

Preparing the Soup:

1. Place the chicken in a large pot. Cover with water (at least 2 qts.). Add the vegetables, bouillon, and pepper, and boil 1 to 1½ hours until the chicken is almost falling off the bones.

2. Add additional bouillon to achieve desired saltiness.

3. Remove the chicken and set it aside.

4. Allow the soup to cool and the grease to rise to the top. Skim it off, saving 1 tablespoon of the fat for the matzo balls.

Making the Matzo Balls:

1. Beat the egg yolks and set aside.

2. Beat the egg whites until stiff and set aside.

3. Fry the celery and onion in the chicken fat until translucent. Near the end, add the garlic.

4. Then add the boiling chicken broth, stir, and allow to cool a few minutes. Stir in the matzo meal, egg yolks, parsley, dill, and baking powder.

5. When evenly mixed, fold in the egg whites, and put in the refrigerator for 1 hour to solidify into a workable dough.

6. Reheat the pot of soup to a rolling boil.

7. Remove the matzo mix from the refrigerator and form heaping tablespoons of the mix into Ping-Pong size balls (no larger) and drop into the boiling soup.

8. Cover and simmer for 30 minutes.

At the last minute, Jodi de-boned the chicken and added some of the meat to the soup. Probably wasn't kosher, but it sure was good!

Serves 8.

Matzo Balls:

2 eggs, separated

1 Tbsp. *schmaltz* (the chicken fat)

1 celery stalk, diced fine

1 small onion, diced fine

2 cloves garlic, diced or crushed

1 cup of the chicken broth (heated to boiling in a saucepan)

1 cup matzo meal

1 Tbsp. fresh parsley, chopped

1 Tbsp. fresh dill (or ½ tsp. dry)

½ tsp. baking powder

Recipes from Book Seven

About the book:

From Thanksgiving and Christmas to rolling in the New Year, the Yada Yadas are "decked out" to celebrate the holidays!

From Jodi's Journal: "Turkey dinners, tree trimming, and decking the halls—it's that time of year again! And I can't wait to celebrate. My kids are coming home for Thanksgiving and Christmas, and then all of us Yadas are getting decked out for a big New Year's party."

However, God's idea of "decked out" just might change the nature of the Yada Yadas' party plans. A perplexing encounter with a former student, a crime that literally knocks Jodi off her feet, a hurry-up wedding that gives all the sisters a glimpse of what the "Christmas story" might look like today, and a child who will forever change the Baxter family . . . it's times like these that a woman really needs her praying sisters.

(*But WAIT! Is this the end of the Yada Yada Prayer Group? Not by a long shot. With Jodi and several other Yadas volunteering at Manna House, a women's shelter in Chicago, the stories just keep popping up, with some new characters thrown in—and we end up with a new series: The Yada Yada House of Hope . . . and the Harry Bentley Books . . .* Lucy Come Home . . . *and then the SouledOut Sisters . . . followed by the Windy City Neighbors series—enough reading for all those long winter nights!*)

Recipes for those winter days:

This holiday season, the Yada Yadas are learning that no one can out-celebrate God.

Even everyday meals on those cold winter nights can become a celebration of God's good care and provision—especially if an unexpected guest shows up and you pull up another chair. Hospitality is what the holidays are all about!

So why don't you join them, try some of these recipes, set an extra place at the table, and get this party started!

Jodi's Hungarian Chicken and Dumplings

Jodi's not Hungarian, but who cares? It's all that paprika! When the weather gets cold, the Baxter clan starts clamoring for chicken and dumplings, the perfect cold-weather comfort food.

1 chicken, cut up, or eight pieces

1 Tbsp. paprika

½ tsp. salt

¼ tsp. black pepper

½ tsp. dried thyme

1 Tbsp. olive oil

2 stalks of celery, split and cut into 3" pieces

4 med. carrots, split and cut into 3" pieces

2 med. onions, quartered

4 cups of chicken stock (or bouillon in water)

Dumplings:

1 ½ cup unbleached flour

1 ½ tsp. baking powder

¼ tsp. salt

3 Tbsp. chopped, fresh parsley (or 3 tsp. dried)

2 Tbsp. vegetable shortening

½ cup milk

1. Rinse the chicken, pat dry, and cover with the paprika, salt, pepper, and thyme, rubbing it in. Sauté the chicken in the oil until brown.

2. Add the vegetables and chicken to the chicken stock and bring it to a boil in a large pot. Simmer for about 30 minutes.

Don't get sidetracked by the phone or the newspaper. You still have to . . .

Make the dumplings:

1. Combine ingredients (reserving some parsley for a garnish) and form into golf-ball-size dumplings.

2. Drop the dumplings into the simmering broth, arranging them so they will expand to cover the surface.

3. Put a lid on your pot and cook for another 15 minutes.

4. Garnish with parsley and serve in bowls to accommodate the juice.

Consider coleslaw or cucumber salad as a side.

Serves 4-6 . . . but don't count on any leftovers.

Estelle's Orange-Smothered Pork Chops

Don't tell anybody, but Estelle accidentally invented this when she had a dab of marmalade she didn't have the heart to throw out, so she threw it on the pork chop she was cooking instead. It was so good, she keeps a jar of marmalade now just for chops.

One pork chop per serving (Select chops about ½ inch thick.)

Corn oil

1 Tbsp. orange marmalade per chop

¼ cup orange juice per chop

Pinch of ground, rubbed sage per chop

A couple dashes of seasoned salt per chop

Fresh-ground black pepper to taste

1. In a skillet large enough to accommodate your chops flat on the bottom, put about 1 Tbsp. of corn oil. (More may be required if your chops are particularly lean.)

2. Cover each chop with the seasoned salt, sage, and pepper.

3. Sear the chops in the skillet over high heat until brown on both sides.

4. Pour off excess grease and allow the pan to cool slightly.

5. Mix the marmalade into the orange juice and pour over chops. Decrease heat and gently simmer for about twenty minutes or until the orange juice thickens to a syrup, turning the chops two or three times. Do not allow the syrup to scorch.

6. Serve on a bed of rice, pouring the juice over the top. Garnish with sprigs of fresh curly parsley. *(And it's okay to puff out your chest and whisper, "Secret recipe," when your family raves. Estelle won't mind.)*

Serves . . . the number of chops you cook.

Ruth's Potato Latkes

Simple to make, kids like them, and they're kosher! (Of course, if you have twins trying to "help" and the phone rings . . . even "simple" has its limits.)

4 medium potatoes

1 medium onion or three scallions, finely chopped

1 tsp. salt

¼ tsp. black pepper

¼ cup fresh parsley, chopped (optional)

¾ cup matzo meal (bread crumbs or 3 Tbsp. flour may be substituted)

2 eggs, beaten

Vegetable oil

1. Grate the potatoes into a large bowl. Discard any liquid. Stir in onions, salt, pepper, and parsley. Add the matzo, mixing well before stirring in the eggs.

2. Heat oil in a large frying pan. Use ¼ to ⅓ cup of batter for each latke, spreading it with a fork into thin cakes about the size of your palm. Cook 4 to 5 minutes per side or until golden brown. Drain pan-fried latkes on paper towels. (Or heat a griddle to 350 degrees with just a spray of oil on it. Griddle latkes may not turn out so crispy, but they contain far less fat.)

3. Serve hot with a scoop of cold applesauce and a dollop of sour cream.

4. If desired, accompany with sausages. *(But don't tell Ruth if they're not kosher.)*

Serves about 4.

Jodi's Flaky Pie Crust

Jodi says, "Can't knit . . . can't sky dive . . . can't dance the light fantastic. But I can make a good pie crust." Denny likes to make her prove it (he has a weakness for pie).

(Jodi's hint: a pie crust that flakes like good pastry is as much technique as right ingredients.)

2 cups flour

1 tsp. salt

⅔ cup vegetable shortening, divided in half

5 to 7 Tbsp. ice water (fill a small bowl with ice cubes, then add water)

1. Cut ⅓ cup shortening into dry ingredients with a pastry blender until well blended.

2. Cut in remaining ⅓ cup shortening.

3. Sprinkle 1 Tbsp. of ice water at a time onto the flour/shortening mixture while you toss it with a fork. Add from 5 to 7 spoonfuls . . . just until dough can be gathered into a ball.

4. Divide dough, slightly more than half for the bottom crust. Roll out dough quickly and gently on a floured counter or board. (Too much handling is what makes it tough.) Pat any tears with a dab of water to stick the dough back together.

5. Turn over once. Dust with flour as needed to roll smoothly to a diameter about 1 inch larger than your pie pan. To transfer a rolled-out pie crust to the pan, roll it up around the rolling pin, then unroll the crust into the pan. Open it and cut off excess, leaving ½ inch extending beyond the edge.

6. Fill with your favorite filling.

For a two-crust pie . . .

1. Repeat the above, and lay second crust over the filling, leaving 1 inch extending beyond the edge. Use a knife or pastry scissors to cut off excess. Tuck top overlap *under* the edge of the bottom crust.

2. Make a fluted edge by pinching the dough edge with thumb and forefinger of the left hand while pushing forefinger of the right hand between the pinch. Continue all around the pie. Cut slits in the top crust to release steam while baking. *(Jodi cuts eyes and mouth to make a happy face. Of course, when the juice dribbles out the slits, it looks like the happy face is either crying or slobbering.)*

Bake at required temperature for the filling (e.g., For apple pie, bake in an oven preheated to 450 degrees for 10 minutes, then turn down the temperature to 350 degrees for about 30 minutes or until the edges of the crust are golden brown).

Florida's Sweet Potato Pie

Florida says, "The recipe below is for one pie, but you better make two! Ya gotta have enough pie for all the drop-ins, know what I'm sayin'?"

2 lbs. or 2 to 3 sweet potatoes
1 stick butter (¼ lb.)
2 eggs
1 cup brown sugar
1 ½ cups soymilk or 1 can evaporated milk
1 tsp. vanilla
1 tsp. cinnamon
1 tsp. nutmeg
½ tsp. ginger
¼ tsp. cloves
¼ tsp. salt
Pie crust (See Jodi's Flaky Pie Crust recipe on precedng page.)

1. Boil the sweet potatoes with the skins on until tender. Cool under running water until you can remove skins. Place the yams in a mixer and whip on medium speed, stopping occasionally to remove "strings" clinging to the beaters.

2. Add butter, until melted and mixed. Then add the remaining ingredients, continue mixing until smooth. If the batter is too thick to pour, add additional soy milk until smooth.

3. Pour your batter into an unbaked pie shell, sprinkle a dash of cinnamon on the top and bake for 50 minutes to 1 hour, or until brown specks appear on the surface of the pie and an inserted knife blade comes out clean.

4. Allow to cool at least 1 hour. It is also delicious chilled.

Serves 6 brothers or 8 "sistahs" on a diet.

Estelle's Holiday Corn Puddin'

Corn pudding?! Never heard of it!" Just smile smugly and tell them Estelle guarantees this will melt in their mouths. It looks pretty, too, with those bits of red and green peppers.

1 can (15 oz.) of creamed corn
3 Tbsp. flour
1 tsp. salt
1 Tbsp. sugar
2 dashes nutmeg
2 dashes black pepper
3 eggs, well beaten
3 Tbsp. melted butter
1 cup milk (for richer flavor, try soy milk)
¼ green bell pepper, finely diced
¼ red bell pepper, finely diced
Paprika

1. Preheat oven to 325 degrees.
2. Combine creamed corn and all dry ingredients, mixing well. Stir in the eggs, butter, and milk. Add the peppers.
3. Pour all ingredients into a greased 1½ quart baking dish.
4. Sprinkle the top with paprika.
5. Bake for 1 hour or until the pudding is firm and a knife comes out clean.

Serves 4 to 6.

US TO METRIC CONVERSION TABLE

CAPACITY

1/5 teaspoon = milliliter
1 teaspoon = 5 milliliters
1 tablespoon = 15 milliliters
1 fluid ounce = 30 milliliters
1/5 cup = 50 milliliters
1 cup = 240 milliliters
2 cups (1 pint) = 470 milliliters
4 cups (1 quart) = .95 liter
4 quarts (1 gallon) = 3.8 liters

WEIGHT

1 ounce = 28 grams
1 pound = 454 grams

Recipe Index

Salads

Soups

Sides

Main Dishes

Desserts

Available in Print and E-book

What's going on

Behind the House of Hope

. . . and Beyond?

Available in Print and E-book from DaveNeta.com

Made in the USA
Monee, IL
27 January 2022